TORAH
FOR HEBREW'S IN EXILE

The Mitzvot's

WHAT IS THE TORAH

BY
Rabbi Robert B. Holman, Jr.

© Copyright 2023 by Printed Page Publishers - All rights reserved.

It is not legal to reproduce, duplicate, or transmit any part of this document in either electronic means or printed format. Recording of this publication is strictly prohibited.

This book is dedicated to:

My late wife Lady Mary D. Holman and my best friend the late Rabbi Robert David Young. Also, to all the Hebrew people in exile dispersed among the nations.

Contents

Introduction..9

CHAPTER ONE
The Virtue Of Miztvot Application.................................19

CHAPTER TWO
Applicable Torah Mitzvots B'reshit (Gen) And Sh'mot (Exo) ..36

CHAPTER THREE
Applicable Torah Mitzvahs Vayikra (Lev).........................49

CHAPTER FOUR
Applicable Mitzvots – Bamidbar (Num)..........................77

CHAPTER FIVE
Applicable Mitzvots D'varim (Deu).................................83

Epilogue/Conclusion..90

Bibliography..92

Acknowledgments 93

About the Author 94

Introduction

I would like to thank those of you who have purchased this writing. My commitment to you through this writing is that it is true and factual. It is based on Scripture and the words of the EL of Hebrew Yisra'el. It is the foundation of having a pure and reliable relationship EL.

Scripture text used in this document is identified in two forms. If it is italicized, it is from the Complete Jewish Bible (CJB) version. If it is not italicized, it is from the New King James (NKJ) version.

As you read this book take note that this writer does not use terminology that suppresses, hides, or covers up the opulence of the creator's name and meaning with language that is not written in the Torah Scroll. The Torah Scroll refers to the Set apart Spirit as YHWH (YAHWEH), YAH, EL, Elohim. Writers of text use God and Lord translated from the Greek language and Hebrew bibles use Adonai which means Lord or Master. Both of these translations dismiss the true text written in the Hebrew Scroll. The Most High's name YAHWEH has been substituted in translations of Scripture to the title "Lord" some 6,823 times. The short form 'YAH' has been translated to Lord 48 times. One place this shows up is Tehillim (Psa) 68:4 *Sing to EL, sing praises to his name; extol him who rides on the clouds by his name, Yah; and be glad in his presence.* Lord and God are not names they are titles. Many people have written books in which they convey the many names of the Most High. But I submit to you those are not his name. They are the titles of what the Set apart Spirit does and/or descriptors that convey his many attributes and abilities.

Concerning the use of the word GOD, in Yeshayahu (Isa) 65:11,12 it says, *"But as for you who abandon YAHWEH, who forget my holy mountain, who prepare a table for a Gad, a god of luck, and fill bowls of mixed wine for Meni, a god of destiny— I will destine you to the sword, you will all bow down to be slaughtered."* There are many words associated with the word God. [C.J. Koster in his book "Come Out of Her My People"] explains in detail the origin and usage of the word used as a substitute for the Father's name YHVH. Here in our text, we see the word Gad is referring to the Hebrew people in the end of days, which we are now in, have forsaken the Mighty One El, YAHWEH to be serving Gad, the

Sun-deity as the deity of "Good Luck, and Meni, the Moon-deity of "Destiny." In C.J. Koster's book he cites the following: "Encyclopedia Britannica, 11th edition, says, "GOD is the common Teutonic word for a personal object of religious worship and applied to all those superhuman beings of heathen mythologies. The word 'god' on the conversion of the Teutonic races to Christianity was adopted as the name of the one Supreme Being. . .." Webster's Twentieth Century Dictionary, Unabridged, 1st edition says, "The word is common to Teutonic tongues. It was applied to heathen deities and later, when the Teutonic people were converted to Christianity, the word was elevated to the Christian sense."] The fact that the word God is shrouded in its origin and also has its association with matters that are heathen, this writer can't use it. Furthermore, another reason is that the word God is a title, and it is not the name of the Mighty One, EL. The Hebrew Scroll never uses the word God in text, it is expressed Hebraically as the Tetragrammaton, YHVH. When using the vowel points it is translated and pronounced YAHWEH, YAHAWAH or YAHUAH without the vowel points. This name is not written in any of the Greek bibles. It is left out.

It is only written in bibles that are Hebraically written, the Complete Jewish Bible, the Scriptures Bible, and the Hebrew Roots Bible. Sh'mot (Exodus) 3:13-15 is transliterated as follows:

> [Moshe said to EL, "Look, when I appear before the people of Yisra'el and say to them, 'The Elohey of your ancestors has sent me to you'; and they ask me, 'What is his name?' what am I to tell them?" EL said to Moshe,"Ehyeh Asher Ehyeh [I am/will be what I am/will be]," and added, "Here is what to say to the people of Yisra'el: 'Ehyeh [I Am, or I Will Be] has sent me to you.'" EL said further to Moshe," Say this to the people of Yisra'el: 'Yud-Heh-Vav-Heh [YAHWEH], the Elohey of your fathers, the Elohey of Avraham, the Elohey of Yitz'chak and the Elohey of Ya'akov, has sent me to you.' **This is my name forever; this is how I am to be remembered generation after generation.**

This transliteration of words is not written in any Greek bibles or bibles authored by Eurocentric people. Because of the afore mentioned historical information this writer does not use a name that is associated with heathenism. This writer expresses the Mighty One's name and not a title. His name is YAHWEH. There is a mitzvot in Sh'mot 23: 13 *"Pay attention to everything I have said to you; do not invoke the names of other gods or even let them be heard crossing your lips."*

Why a book like this? This writer taught Torah based on the Ashkenazi view for many years. In their view the Torah Parashah loop portions, readings, and teachings have been the weekly emphasis. That taught me about culture, the establishment of Hebrew Yisra'el and many other understandings. While Torah lives within the first five books, the Ashkenazi never singled out that the one most important single study is knowing and understanding Torah. That Torah are rules, regulations, and instructions that should be the central focus of study. Now that I know, I want to share this information especially with those who are a part of YAHWEH'S Exiled Empire. The exiled Hebrew Yisra'el people and all who want to know and live their lives accordingly. It is important for people who are gravitating to the Hebraic way of life to have and know the most single issue that will solidly connect them to the EL of Avraham, Yitz'chak, and Ya'akov. The single most narrative that you will read in Hebrew Scripture is the directive from YAHWEH the EL of Yisra'el is to **OBEY** the Torah.

In this writing you will learn what the Torah is, and which of these mitzvot are to be adhered to in this exile. Reading this book will help every Hebrew Yisra'lite in exile to know their responsibility to the EL of Hebrew Yisra'el throughout all their generations. This writing is not intended to be conclusive of applicable mitzvots for people in exile. As you read the Hebrew writings of scripture you may find some mitzvots that you determine to be applicable.

Torah, what is it? To the Ashkenazi Jews, as well as most people who don't know, it is referred to as the first five books of Scripture. To Hebrew Yisra'el it is referred to as the Law of Moshe. Moshe called them the laws and rulings to live by and follow. They are the governance by which the nation of Hebrew Yisra'el walks and lives in harmony with the EL, the Mighty One, throughout all generations wherever Hebrew Yisra'el lives. These laws, rules, and teachings live within the five books from B'reshit (Gen) to D'varim (Deu).

The main reason Hebrew Yisra'el is in diaspora out of the land which flowed with milk and honey is because our ancestors failed to live by the Torah of Moshe. How important is it? Well, take time to read Vayikra (Lev) Chapter 26 and D'varim (Num) 28:15-69 you will see how important the Torah is to Hebrew Yisra'el. There is only one people who fit the narrative of these two texts, and it is Hebrew Yisra'el in exile, the myelinated people. Here is what the writer of Lamentations 5:7 says, *"Our ancestors sinned and no longer exist; we bear the weight of their guilt." We are ruled by slaves, and there is no one to save us from their power.*

In Tehillim (Psalms) 97:11 it says that *"Light is sown for the righteous and joy for the upright in heart."* Then in Mishlie (Proverbs) 1:8-9 it states, *"My son, heed the discipline of your father [YAHWEH], and do not abandon the teaching of your mother [your nation]; they will be a garland to grace your head, a medal of honor for your neck."* I present these two texts because they express the fact that the Torah is the light of being set apart through which a person draws close to YAHWEH. When we look closely at the Torah. It attaches a commandment to virtually every activity of life. The absence of Torah principles can lead us to become preoccupied with material pursuits. It is material pursuits that makes it easy for one to forget that our primary allegiance is to YAHWEH.

The writer of Mishlie (Proverbs) states that they (mitzvots) are a garland to grace the neck if you heed the discipline of your father a reference to YAHWEH and the written and oral law given to Moshe. The reference to your mother in Proverbs is directed to the nation of Yisra'el as a whole; so, heed the discipline of the written and the oral law given by YAHWEH to Moshe and the teaching of your mother the nation of Yisra'el. In so doing the mitzvot's will be a garland to grace you head, a medal of honor for your neck. There is a mitzvot for every aspect of life to help us to stay focused on our Savior and King, YAHWEH, so that we don't get so caught up in a life built on materialism. Yeshayahu (Isa) 44:6,7 *Thus says YAHWEH, Yisra'el's King and Redeemer, YAHWEH -Tzva'ot [of Host]: "I am the first, and I am the last; besides me there is no EL. Who is like me? Let him speak out! Let him show me clearly what has been happening since I set up the eternal people; let him foretell future signs and events.* Yeshayahu (Isa) 48:17,18 *Thus says YAHWEH, your Redeemer, the Holy One of Yisra'el: "I am YAHWEH, your EL, who teaches you for your own good, who guides you on the path you should take. If only you would heed my mitzvot! Then your peace would flow on like a river, and your righteousness like the waves of the sea.*

The question might be, "why was the Torah given to Hebrew Yisra'el as a nation?" We must look at D'varim (Deu.) 33:2 it says, *"YAHWEH came from Sinai; from Se'ir he dawned on his people, shone forth from Mount Pa'ran; and with him were myriads of holy ones; at his right hand was a fiery law for them."* What this means is the Torah was not offered to the Hebrew people first. It was offered to Esav and Yishmael. However, they were not suited for the Torah and therefore rejected it. It was our nation of people, Hebrew Yisra'el, who agreed to accept the Torah. YAHWEH knew that all the other nations would reject Torah. Out of all mankind, the fewest of all, Hebrew Yisra'el chose to accept Torah. YAHWEH chose only one people: the people of Hebrew Yisra'el.

The myriad of spirits, YAHWEH's servants who are intrinsically set apart are always ready and waiting to perform good acts in the service of YAHWEH. When we look at their nature it does not afford them the possibility of sinning. Ezekiel 1:9 says, *"they never stray form their path."* Know this the words of the Torah are not directed at them. The Torah is designed to lay down the life regimen for spiritual-physical creatures who are called upon to obey YAHWEH in freedom. Neither Se'ir Esav nor Pa'ran Yishmael were suited for the Torah as their eternal lifestyles would be averse to the "Most High", EL and they knew this.

In the text above D'varim (Deu) 33:2 is the Hebrew word (dat) which means fiery law. It's a Dalet (ד) and a tav (ת) and it only occurs here as a term that defines the concept of the Torah.

It is the cosmic conception of the Torah, and it designates the Torah's significance in YAHWEH's universal scheme. This Torah governs man as we are called upon to exercise moral freedom. However, this Torah does not operate within us, without our knowledge and without our will; it comes to us, so that we may accept it in the freedom of our mind and will. We must realize that the Torah is nothing but YAHWEH's laws addressed to man, which in all creatures operates automatically. In other words, every aspect of creation operates in accordance with the laws that govern their existence. Yet man is given the right to choose or reject to fulfill the laws of the "Most High", El. When we do, we do so consciously and freely. This is what all other creatures do unconsciously and freely. The Torah is the "Fire transformed into the Law."

In verse 4 of the text in D'varim 33 it says, *"the Torah Moshe commanded us as an inheritance for the community of Ya'akov."* Verse four allows us to know that the Torah is the heritage for Hebrew Yisra'el. It was given to Hebrew Yisra'el and not any other nation.

Listen to what Moshe says in D'varim (Deu) 7:6-9 *6 For you are a people Set apart as Set apart for YAHWEH Eloheycha (your El)). YAHWEH Eloheycha (your El) has chosen you out of all the peoples on the face of the earth to be his own unique treasure. 7 YAHWEH didn't set his heart on you or choose you because you numbered more than any other people—on the contrary, you were the fewest of all peoples. 8 Rather, it was because YAHWEH loved you, and because he wanted to keep the oath which he had sworn to your ancestors, that YAHWEH brought you out with a strong hand and redeemed you from a life of slavery under the hand of Pharaoh king of Egypt. (Maftir) 9 From this you can know that YAHWEH Eloheycha (your EL) is indeed EL, the faithful El, who keeps his covenant and extends grace to those who love him and observe his mitzvot, to a thousand generations."* How many generations? A thousand generations. So how can they be done away?

Take note of the language of this text. You are set apart for YAHWEH. YAHWEH has chosen you out of all the peoples on the face of the earth, the nation is his own unique treasure, it is because he loves us. Hey, you, Moshe is telling us what he knows about the set apart Spirit. The Nation of Hebrew Yisra'el is special to the "Most High", EL; that is why we have these mitzvot, laws, and instructions. We should not take them lightly. Let the other nations and even our Hebrew brethren who are attached to the nations, do whatever they please. Just know that our refuge, pure Hebrew Yisra'el, is in our obedience to what our EL has instructed us to do.

Does the all-wise eternal Spirit know the end from the beginning? The answer is yes. Scripture validates that we accepted his Torah by saying, "all that you have said we will do." Nothing concerning the Most High is an afterthought nor does it arise within a different time. It has already been established before the framing of the world.

This study will help you to understand that the Torah is the only means by which man can come to know his creator. YAHWEH created man to be a corporal creature with a sense of spirituality. Man serves to make known that nothing is impossible to YAHWEH. We are a blend of substance and spirit which are complete opposites. However, YAHWEH blended the two through his great wisdom and created man out of them. Without the Torah we would be completely drawn toward substance in the fulfillment of all our physical desires and we would be likened and compared to animals. The giving of the Torah is essential to enlighten the hearts of people which is essential to the perfection of creation.

What you will come to realize by reading this book is that by adhering to Torah it can have a positive effect on one's life in this world and the world to come.

The one main text that supports this writing and puts it into perspective are these words which the Most High spoke in Bamidbar (Num) 15:15 *For this community there will be the same law for you as for the foreigner living with you;* **_this is a permanent regulation through all your generations_**; *the foreigner is to be treated the same way before YAHWEH as yourselves. The same Torah and standard of judgment will apply to both you and the foreigner living with you.'"* Question: Can anything that the Mighty One, El, YAHWEH spoke as being permanent be changed? Answer: No! How long is through all your generations? Get the picture?

Key Takeaway

Malachi 3:22 *"Remember the Torah of Moshe my servant, which I enjoined on him at Horev, laws and rulings for all Yisra'el."*

NOTES:

CHAPTER ONE

THE VIRTUE OF MIZTVOT APPLICATION

D'varim 4:1 and 2 *"Now, Yisra'el, listen to the laws and rulings I am teaching you, in order to follow them, so that you will live; . . . obey the mitzvot of YAHWEH your EL which I am giving you, do not add to what I am saying, and do not subtract from it."*

The way we can nurture our bodies and keep it spiritually alive and healthy is by adhering to the laws, instructions, and commandments/mitzvots exactly as the Torah explains them.

The positive commandments are physically performed by the organs of the body and give us an opportunity to elevate ourselves and increase our position in the Messianic Era. Torah prohibitions are referred to as negative commandments which are meant to prevent us from losing our share or position in the Messianic Era. There is little to no teaching in Christendom concerning the Messianic Era. It is the time frame that is germane to Hebrew Yisra'el's redemption also known as the seventh day. This is the time when Hebrew Yisra'el will be redeemed back into the land. It is referred to as the Messianic Era because it is at this time that Hebrew Yisra'el's true anointed one will be revealed. As such, we are currently experiencing the sixth day called the day of grace.

Why is there a time of grace? I submit to you that all of the laws, rules, teachings, and instructions given to Hebrew Yisra'el were deemed for a nation and people who lived in the set apart land. In that land they had a King, Temple, Cohanim, and Livi'im to carry out every aspect of Torah as directed by the "Most High" EL. The "Most High" El knew that with his people in diaspora to the nations they would not be able to fulfill some of the mitzvots. So, YAHWEH extended grace. As you read through Scripture you will find that some of the mitzvots demand death for Hebrew Yisra'el's failure to comply. But YAHWEH has given to the nation during this time frame his grace.

When I think about the revelation that is before me and how the mitzvots are connected to life. I realize that YAHWEH created the body as the garment for the soul, to correspond to the spiritual contours of the soul. When YAHWEH breathed the soul into the body it was to bring the body to life and activate the body to perform the commandments. This is because Torah was intended for *human* beings with bodies, passions, and interactions.

I am now better able to understand physical life and breath. Also, man is faced with the contrasting of good and evil. The pure soul inhabits the body and so does an impure spiritual source, the evil inclination. Our soul is nourished by our observance of the commandments and the nourishment of the evil inclination is the opposite. The thing that makes Torah and the mitzvots so important to us is that when we fail to uphold the mitzvots, set apartness oozes out of the soul of man and it is as if the spiritual arteries become clogged and the spiritual limbs become atrophied or begin to waste away. Our physical bodies may continue to function, but it may become drained of its set apart, life-force which is connected to the life to come.

Everything associated with the creation and the domain of man is spiritual in essence. This is because all creation is the work of the Set Apart Spirit. It is a known fact that man was placed in the garden of Eden to cultivate and care for it. The commandment given to man was simple. Just cultivate and care for the land. This was a commandment from the Creator. If we stop and think about the Garden of Eden, things did not start to happen until man arrived. YAHWEH planted seeds; however, its success was dependent upon man's hand to protect and guard them. Land becomes barren if not properly tended to and humanity will not arrive at its intended goal without the direction of the Set Apart Spirit. Therefore, the creator provided man with instructions to enable and accomplish both tasks. The governance of the land and the development of the human soul. You see spirituality is the underlying essence of all human and material existence. Both require active work and protection to thrive.

With this view in mind, we must consider what affect our doing the commandments have on us. They produce growth for us on earth and in the world to come. So, we do good by obeying YAHWEH'S commandments. The mitzvots cannot be set aside just because Eurocentric men do not understand or know our EL. Nor can they tell us what we can and cannot do as it pertains to the mandates from our EL.

The Prophet Hosea says these words in chapter 10:2 *"If you sow righteousness for yourselves, you will reap according to grace. Break up unused ground for yourselves, because it is time to seek YAHWEH, till he comes and rains down righteousness upon you."* What does this mean? This speaks to the point of obtaining righteousness which can only be garnered through Torah's application to one's life. Hosea continues the thought that the person seeking YAHWEH'S righteousness needs to break up his reluctance to seek the knowledge of YAHWEH. Now is the time to seek YAHWEH until he rains down righteousness upon us (Here "rain" is a metaphor for Torah).

In the realm of spirituality, our success in this body and in life depends upon how we adapt to YAHWEH'S rule. How does our body correspond to obeying YAHWEH'S mitzvots? Let's hear what the Psalmist has to say in Psalms 1:14 *"I thank you because I am awesomely made, wonderfully; your works are wonders— I know this very well. 15 My bones were not hidden from you when I was being made in secret, intricately woven in the depths of the earth. 16 Your eyes could see me as an embryo, but in your book all my days were already written; my days had been shaped before any of them existed."* Psalms 119:73 *"Your hands made and formed me;* **give me understanding, so I can learn your mitzvot.** *74 Those who fear you rejoice at the sight of me, because I put my hope in your word. 75 I know,* **YAHWEH, that your rulings are righteous**, *that even when you humble me you are faithful. 76 Let your grace comfort me, in keeping with your promise to your servant."* Psalms 119:77 *"Show me pity, and* **I will live, for your Torah is my delight**. *78 Let the proud be ashamed, because they wrong me with lies as for me,* **I will meditate on your precepts.** *79 Let those who fear you turn to me, along with those who know your* **instruction**. **80 Let my heart be pure in your laws**, *so that I won't be put to shame."*

Earthly existence has two components; one is beneath the sun the other is above the sun. Ecc 1:3 *What does a person gain from all his labor at which he toils under the sun? 4 Generations come, generations go, but the earth remains forever. 5 The sun rises, the sun sets; then it speeds to its place and rises there.* There are many things that come and go. But YAHWEH's words embodied in the Torah are from generation to generation.

When we see that the Most High created the heavens, they are a stark witness to what YAHWEH has done and continues to do. A true study of the stars finds that the names of the twelve sons of Yisra'el are numbered within the constellations. The sun symbolizes control of physical activity and the Torah's prohibitions correspond to the days of the solar year. Torah compliant people must never commit a sin that will reduce their stature. The sun's role is to maintain the equilibrium of our solar system by never varying its orbit and the force of gravity. We too must be protected from decline and the Torah's prohibitions accomplish that protection. What we must take to heart is that it's a 365-day pursuit. Just as the sun takes no vacation, we too must be diligent in our pursuit to accomplish obedience to the mitzvots.

Christian narrative would call this legalism. However, it is out of love for the one who has created us that we begin to realize the significances of applying the mitzvots to our life. There must be an understanding of the significance to our obedience to the mitzvots and why they are so meaningful to Hebrews in exile. It is due to the pureness of intent of the heart and soul of the Hebrew in Exile to adhere to the many times in scripture text that our EL admonishes us to **OBEY**. D'varim (Deu) 7:6-9. *For you are a people Set apart as Set apart for YAHWEH Eloheycha (your El). YAHWEH Eloheycha has chosen you out of all the peoples on the face of the earth to be his own unique treasure. 7 YAHWEH didn't set his heart on you or choose you because you numbered more than any other people— on the contrary, you were the fewest of all peoples. 8 Rather, it was because YAHWEH loved you, and because he wanted to keep the oath which he had sworn to your ancestors, that YAHWEH brought you out with a strong hand and redeemed you from a life of slavery under the hand of Pharaoh king of Egypt. (Maftir) 9 From this you can know that YAHWEH Eloheycha is indeed EL, the faithful El, who keeps his covenant and extends grace to those who love him and observe his mitzvot, to a thousand generations.'*

While we have been told that the Law of Moshe, the Torah, or the Law is not for us, it is important to understand what Sha'ul (Paul) is saying in Romans 6:14 (Greek text) "For sin shall not have dominion over you: for ye are not under the law, but under grace"; Hebrew text says it correctly *"For sin will not have authority over you; because you are not under legalism but under grace."* He is saying that in his day the Pharisees and Sadducees had written policy or what in Hebraic terms is called a "fence" to guard the application of Torah obedience and there with they taught their perverted policy, called the perversion of the Torah, instead of pure Torah. Therefore, we are not to follow these perversions, such as the Talmud, or the Mishna but follow Torah as it was given to the Hebrew people by Moshe without their meriting it thusly Grace. I appeal to the golden rule of the Most High El in D'varim (Deu) 4:2 *"do not add to what I am saying, and do not subtract from it."* D'varim (Deu) 13:1 *"Everything I am commanding you, you are to take care to do. Do not add to it or subtract from it.*

The Torah Personality

The total Torah personality is symbolized in an individual whose behavior reflects all facets of Torah fulfillment, that is both in his personality and relationship with YAHWEH and his relationship with his fellowman.

The role of character development is an integral component in the spiritual growth process of the Torah compliant Hebrew and a key to the emergence of the Hebrew people as the ethical Torah personality. This being said, we come to realize that the Law, Torah, is not only ethical but it is also filled with moral trait building concepts. Concepts that when applied to the life of the Hebrew in exile, the righteousness in which the Creator, YAHWEH, desires are manifested. The prophet Yirmeyahu (Jer) 9:22. (23) *Here is what YAHWEH says: "The wise man should not boast of his wisdom, the powerful should not boast of his power, the wealthy should not boast of his wealth; (24) instead, let the boaster boast about this: that he understands and knows me— that I am YAHWEH, practicing grace, justice and righteousness in the land; for in these things I take pleasure," says YAHWEH.*

As mentioned previously Greek text says, we are not under the Law; and Eurocentric commentators say that Jesus fulfilled the Law, so we don't have to pay attention to it. But there is a problem with this premise. The Greek text in 1 John 3:4 says, "Whoever commits sin also commits lawlessness, and sin is lawlessness." The Hebrew text says, *"Everyone who keeps sinning is violating Torah—indeed, sin is violation of Torah."* If we look up the word lawlessness (anomia) in the W.E. Vine Expository Dictionary it says "(unlawful)" where the thought is not simply that of doing what is unlawful, but of flagrant defiance of the known EL." Who is the known EL? None other than the Creator whose name written in the Hebrew text is YAHWEH. So, Vines says that lawlessness is a flagrant defiance of the Set Apart Spirit. The Greeks use the word "Law" and Law is Torah. Therefore, by not obeying the Law, <u>the Greek text says a person commits sin</u>.

This presents a dichotomy, a division or contrast between two things that are or are represented as being opposed or entirely different. It generates confusion in the minds of the people as to what is true and correct.

It is interesting that many religious people say that they have been saved from sin. But then the Greek text says, 1John 1:8 If we say that we have no sin, we deceive ourselves, and the truth is not in us. 9 If we confess our sins, he (Jesus Christ) is faithful and just to forgive us our sins, and to cleanse us from all unrighteousness. 10 If we say that we have not sinned, we make him (Jesus Christ) a liar, and his word is not in us. This text is confusing at best. If being Torah-less or Lawless according to 1John 3:4 makes one a sinner which is why if we say we have no sin, we deceive ourselves. It is the abstinence of a Torah/Law complaint life which is sin. If we confess our Torah-lessness/Lawlessness, he (Jesus) is faithful to forgive us our sin (Torah-lessness/Lawlessness) and to cleanse us from all unrighteousness (Torah-less/Lawless) life. To confess is to acknowledge our Torah-less/Lawless lifestyle and take up living one's life accordingly. If a person is not doing that my question is can Jesus forgive you for something that the Most High EL ask us to do in order to be righteous and without sin? This text in 1John suggest that by ones conforming to Jesus he takes away this Torah/lawless condition. That the person who lives in Christ does not continue in the practice of sin. If that be true, then why do all Christians live a lawless life by violating all of the Divine Law/Torah? Because they have been taught a dichotomy. That the Torah/Law does not apply to them. Christ nailed it to the cross. If that is the case, why did they write this text in 1John 3:4.

Is the Torah Good?

It is a known fact that the Torah of Moshe is moral and ethical. But let us hear what the Most High has to say through his King, King David in Tehillim (Psa) 19:8-11. *(7) The Torah of YAHWEH is **perfect**, restoring the inner person. The instruction of YAHWEH is **sure**, making wise the thoughtless. (8) The precepts of YAHWEH are **right**, rejoicing the heart. The mitzvah of YAHWEH is **pure**, enlightening the eyes. (9) The fear of YAHWEH is **clean**, enduring forever. The rulings of YAHWEH are **true**, they are righteous altogether, (10) more desirable than gold, than much fine gold, also sweeter than honey or drippings from the honeycomb. (11) Through them your servant is warned; **in obeying them there is great reward**.* There is no substitute or replacement for Torah in the life of the Hebrew believer. It does not matter what version of the Scriptures you read; the prior text is going to express the positivity of the Law of Moshe, the Torah, given to him by the Set Apart Spirit YAHWEH.

Hebrews Chapter 7

One of the most repulsive texts concerning the Torah of the Law of Moshe is written in Hebrews Chapter 7:18. Let's hear what the Greeks have to say about the Law of Moshe. I'm going to state the text from a Greek writing then from the Hebrew. "For on the one hand there is an annulling of the former commandment because of its weakness and unprofitableness, for the law made nothing perfect; on the other hand, there is the bringing in of a better hope, through which we draw near to God." Now here is the Hebrew rendering of the same text. *"Thus, on the one hand, the earlier rule is set aside because of its weakness and inefficacy (for the Torah did not bring anything to the goal); and, on the other hand, a hope of something better is introduced, through which we are drawing near to EL."* The Hebrew text is a copy of the Greek text except that it uses Hebrew terminology, nevertheless, it is still egregious. If 2 Timothy 3:16 says, *"All Scripture is EL-breathed and is valuable for teaching the truth, convicting of sin, correcting faults and training in right living; thus, anyone who belongs to God may be fully equipped for every good work."* In Timothy the testimony here is that the scriptures are valuable for teaching truth. We just read in Psalms 19 how the Law or Torah is valuable. But now suddenly it is weak and inefficacy. That what the "Most High", the Set Apart Spirit, YAHWEH gave to Moshe for the Hebrew people was weak and unprofitable is an egregious statement. So, the "Most High" failed? Really? I'm sorry but that is a repulsive thought. There is no failure in the Mighty One EL. But, if the Christians believe and teach that Jesus Christ fulfilled the law so that man no longer needs to abide by it, then He himself is weak and inefficacy. Hmmmmm! I want you to think about this. The writer of Hebrews says what EL gave to us was weak and unprofitable. I know I'm repeating myself, but I want you to really think about this. There is nothing about the Creator EL that is weak and unprofitable. Nothing that He spoke to Moshe, or the Prophets was weak and especially unprofitable. EL does not lie or change his mind; and everything the opulent Spirit did was good and very good. So, do you get my point! Text says, these words in D'varim (Deu) 30:19-20 *"I call on heaven and earth to witness against you today that I have presented you with life and death, the blessing and the curse. Therefore, choose life, so that you will live, you and your descendants, loving YAHWEH your EL, paying attention to what he says and clinging to him— for that is the purpose of your life! On this depends the length of time you will live in the land YAHWEH swore he would give to your ancestors Avraham, Yitz'chak and Ya'akov."* While the text speaks about Kena'ani the text applies to everywhere we live in the world. This is because the Torah is everlasting and throughout generations. When we look at the rules and instructions that YAHWEH gave to Moshe to teach Yisra'el many of them state wherever you live. How important are the mitzvots to Hebrew Yisra'el? Here is what the Prophet Yirmeyahu (Jer) 31: 35 says, "If these laws leave my presence," says, YAHWEH "then the offspring of Yisra'el will stop being a nation in my presence forever." That says that these rules laws and instructions cannot be done away with.

What is Torah or the Law?

I was reading one-night in Tehillim (Psa) 119 when the Ruach the Set Apart Spirit opened my eyes. After years of studying and teaching everything from B'reshit (Gen) to D'varim (Deu) I thought I was teaching Torah by teaching the Ashkenazi Torah Parashah's. I realized that I missed totally what it means to teach Torah. As I read, I started to ask questions. What is King David talking about in the text. Like what **way**, what **instructions**, what **precepts,** what **laws**, what **regulations?** Then he said, "I will not forget your **word.**" I began to ask what these are and where do I find them? It seemed to me that King David was enamored with these matters. I, like you over the many years of reading Scripture never stopped to ask these questions. But now I'm curious to know what they are. I turned to a Scripture text in D'varim (Deu) 4:1 and there it was as plain as day:

> *"Now, Yisra'el, listen to the **laws** and **rulings** I am teaching you, in order to follow them, so that you will live; then you will go in and take possession of the land that YAHWEH, the Elohey of your fathers, is giving you. In order to **obey the mitzvot** of YAHWEH your Eloheychem which I am giving you, do not add to what I am saying, and do not subtract from it. . . . " Look, I have taught you **laws** and **rulings**, just as YAHWEH my Elohey ordered me, so that you can behave accordingly in the land where you are going in order to take possession of it. **Therefore, observe them; and follow them**; for then all peoples will see you as having wisdom and understanding. When they hear of all these **laws**, they will say, 'This great nation is surely a wise and understanding people.' For what great nation is there that has EL as close to them as YAHWEH our Eloheynu is, whenever we call on him? What great nation is there that has **laws and rulings** as just as this entire Torah which I am setting before you today?"*

When I read this then I knew that for all these years what I thought was Torah was simply a history of the Hebrew people. But inside that history resided these laws and rulings of the Most High called mitzvots and commandments. That is when I realized and understood what Torah was. Once I finally understood I started looking for teachings that reflected these laws and rulings by any Torah teacher. I found that nobody was specifically teaching them. Armed with this information I found in my library a list of mitzvots comprised by different Rabbis. Also in my library was a set of books which contained the mitzvots distributed and annotated by ArtScroll the Jewish book vender. I read through all of their material trying to map it to the other sources that I had. I found that none of them agreed. One list of 613 was different from the other. The Ashkenazi's say that there are 613 mitzvahs. All their Rabbis agree with that number. Then I asked myself where in text does the EL of Hebrew Yisra'el tell us that there are 613? Nowhere in Hebrew text does the Most High El enumerate the mitzvots. Not having any agreement from source material, I began reading through text beginning at B'reshit (Gen) looking for every place where the Most High gave a ruling, law, or instruction. After compiling what I found, I realized that the number of them didn't matter. Whether there were more or less than 613 was not important. What was important to the Most High is that Hebrew Yisra'el know them and govern their lives by them, and the number does not matter. The common narrative from the Most High is to "**Obey**" them. In Mattiyahu 7:12 YeShua says, "Therefore, whatever you want men to do to you, do also to them, for this is the Law and the Prophets." Our Hebrew text says, *"Always treat others as you would like them to treat you; that sums up the teaching of the Torah and the Prophets.* Do you notice anything ambiguous. If we are not supposed to be subject to the Law, why is YeShua responding in this manner by indicating that it is by the Law and the Prophets that we are able to function rightly with each other. This is not the only place in the Greek text where they mention adherence to the Law or Torah. Let's see what Sha'ul (Paul) says in Act 24:14-16 *"But this I do admit to you: I worship the EL of our fathers in accordance with the Way (which they call a sect). I continue to believe everything that accords with the Torah,* (LAW) *and everything written in the Prophets. And I continue to have a hope in EL—which they too accept—that there will be a resurrection of both the righteous and the unrighteous. Indeed, it is because of this that I make a point of always having a clear conscience in the sight of both EL and man.* It is also expressed in Romans 4:7 NKJV ""Blessed are those whose <u>*lawless*</u> deeds are forgiven, whose sins are covered; Blessed is the man to whom the LORD shall not impute sin." NKJV 1John 3:4 Whoever commits sin also commits **lawlessness**, and sin is **lawlessness**. In the CJB this same verse reads: 1Yochanan (John) 3:4 *Everyone* *who keeps sinning is violating Torah—indeed, sin is violation of Torah.* When you read the Greek New Testament, you will see this word "law" in lower case and in "LAW" uppercase. It does not matter the word in Hebrew still means Torah, laws, instructions, and commandments. The one point is to dispel that the Torah or LAW given to the nation of Hebrew Yisra'el has not been done away with as the Christian order decrees.

I hope you can see how twisted the Greeks and the Eurocentric commentators are when it comes to the matter of the Torah/Law or for that fact scripture in general. There is only one source of truth, and it resides in the Hebrew Scroll with proper transliteration.

I submit to you that from whatever bible you are reading there is gross error due to the lack of proper transliteration from the Hebrew Scroll. The Greeks have left out text that is germane to understanding and pertinent to the very soul along with their miss application of Hebrew text. The Prophets are grossly misinterpreted. Everywhere they (the Greeks) say this was done to fulfill a prophesy. When you go back and read the pretext and post text reference, there is no correlation to any text the Greeks insert. I should point out that history records that Eurocentric commentaries from which Christian's study are part and parcel the works of medieval Eurocentric authors. These commentaries have been passed down as works of their fathers. These people have no clue about the mitzvots or their application to any Hebrew text. As we look at the mitzvots which the Most High has given to us there is no scripture more important than those which state the mitzvot. If the Most High says something is to be carried throughout all your generations, then the question you must ask is when do generations stop? They don't! When the Most High says we are to '**OBEY**' His rulings, Laws, regulations, and instructions then who should we His people believe and what should we do? Should we believe Eurocentric commentators or what is written in the

Scroll of Hebrew Yisra'el. We are an opulent nation of people in exile with the best governance in the world. This statement belongs to Hebrew Yisra'el. We are the only nation who can rightfully claim this as be true. We are "One nation under El with liberty and justice for all." This is because what the Father gave us is just and right.

As you begin this study of the mitzvots you will realize that the totality of the mitzvots applies to different aspects of our government. Some will apply only to Kohanim while others will apply to non-Kohanim, some to a king and others to us. Some will only apply when in the Land and the Beis HaMikdash or when the Temple is standing during the Messianic Era. This writing of Torah application is only going to address the mitzvots that apply to Hebrew Yisra'el in this exile. The nation in exile is without a King, Temple, or Kohanim. Therefore, the mitzvots mentioned in this writing are moral and ethical and applicable in this exile.

The King David in Tehillim (Psa) 119:15 says, *"I will meditate on your precept and keep my eyes on your ways. I will find my delight in your regulations. I will not forget your word."* I pose a question to you? How can you meditate on something of which you do not know or have any knowledge? You can't. You should read through this whole Psalm and as you do, ask the question what are these laws, precepts, and regulations that King David refers to here. Yes, and bind them always on your heart. For they shall be life to you.

In this writing I am not going to list them by number because you may want to compare and affix a number to them. The number is not the important issue. **OBEYING** them is the primary issue. This grouping will only contain laws and instructions that tend to apply to us in this exile.

You might ask yourself why are these important now to us while in these exiled nations? Because knowing and adhering to these laws and instructions in exile is critical to our teshuvah (repentance). Repentance is the means by which the Hebrew nation in exile can be redeemed sooner than later. What is the act of repentance? It is turning back to and adhering to the Torah. I arrive at this conclusion by understanding the book of Shoftim (Judges). In that historical book we see that YAHWEH raised up judges who would rescue them from the power of those who were plundering them. In every case Hebrew Yisra'el did what was evil from YAHWEH'S perspective. They forgot YAHWEH their EL and served ba'alim (Phoenician deity) and asherim (a Canaan goddess of fortune & happiness; a symbol of this goddess, a *sacred tree* or *pole* set up near an altar). To the Most High these are idols. Any worship given or expressed to any entity or so-called deity other than the opulent Spirit is idolatry.

In the book of Shoftim (Judges) the text says, *"But when the people of Yisra'el cried out to YAHWEH, YAHWEH raised up for them a savior."* The act of crying out is the act of teshuvah, repentance, turning back to the rules and instructions, and mitzvots of the Most High. Hebrew Yisra'el in exile is oppressed by the nations to which they have been exiled. When the pressure of the oppressors become more than Hebrew Yisra'el can bare in this exile, they will do the same as our ancestors; they will cry out. They will turn back to the EL of Avraham, Yitz'chak, and Ya'akov and to the Most High's rules and instructions. But why wait and put off turning back to his rules and instructions. The Most High says in D'varim (Deu) 6: 17,18 17 *Observe diligently the mitzvot of YAHWEH your EL, and his instructions and laws which he has given you. You are to do what is right and good in the sight of YAHWEH,* ***so that things will go well with you.*** That's right in this exile amid everything you and I witness good and bad, yet things can go well for us when we obey the Most High. But what does that mean? It means that the EL of Avraham, Yitz'chak and Ya'akov must honor his word to us. In Tehillim (Psa) 33:4

For the word of YAHWEH is true. In this same book Chapter 37: 3-5 he says, *Trust in YAHWEH, and do good; settle in the land, and feed on faithfulness. Then you will delight yourself in YAHWEH, and he will give you your heart's desire. Commit your way to YAHWEH; trust in him, and he will act.* This is how change comes about in the life of the Hebrew believer. It is by obedience to YAHWEH'S words. One's life can be full and abundant when we obey the teachings of our EL YAHWEH. All of the Most High's work is trustworthy.

Why now and why in this exile is Torah so important? Allow me to explain. The soul of man is the hard drive of man, and it never dies. The soul of man will be awakened from the dust. Daniel 12:2,3 *Many of those sleeping in the dust of the earth will awaken, some to everlasting life and some to everlasting shame and abhorrence. But those who can discern will shine like the brightness of heaven's dome, and those who turn many to righteousness like the stars forever and ever.* Case in point you can take an old hard drive or one that has been lying dormant out of an old computer. You can connect it to new cables in a new computer and it is revived everything on it can be revealed. I believe it is the same with the soul. When we are revived from the dust as we die so are we revived. The things that we have garnered in this life germane to the things of the Most High will manifest in our resurrection in the land. Things there will not be foreign to us. But also, it is by our obedience that the Most High El is as close to us as YAHWEH our El is, whenever we call on him D'varim 4:7?

Chapter Summary/Key Takeaways

TEHILLIM (PSALMS) *119:1:4 You laid down your precepts for us to observe with care. 5 May my ways be steady in observing your laws.*

NOTES:

CHAPTER TWO

APPLICABLE TORAH MITZVOTS B'RESHIT (GEN) AND SH'MOT (EXO)

To procreate and rule.

They begin in B'reshit (Gen) 1:28 *"EL blessed them: EL said to them, "Be fruitful, multiply, fill the earth and subdue it. Rule over the fish in the sea, the birds in the air and every living creature that crawls on the earth."*

Purpose: Is that man engage in procreation to populate the world. Where there exist man and woman cohabiting together, we should endeavor to fulfill this mitzvot of procreation, because the fulfilling of it is not in one's control, as various factors can prevent one from having children. This mitzvot is incumbent more on the man than the woman due to the many complications she may have that may prevent her from childbirth as was Sarah and Na'omi's case that without YAHWEH's intervention these women may have never had children. However, while it is incumbent upon the male, the woman is the conduit by which the birth is produced.

Keeping the Sabbath.

B'reshit (Gen) 2:1-3 *"Thus the heavens and the earth were finished, along with everything in them. On the seventh day God was finished with his work which he had made, so he rested on the seventh day from all his work which he had made. God blessed the seventh day and separated it as holy; because on that day God rested from all his work which he had created, so that it itself could produce."* This verse establishes what Hebrew Yisra'el is supposed to do regarding the Sabbath. YAHWEH establishes the precedent for our obedience. Sh'mot (Ex)31:12-17 *"YAHWEH said to Moshe, "Tell the people of Yisra'el, 'You are to observe my Shabbats; for this is a sign between me and you through all your generations; so that you will know that I am YAHWEH, who sets you apart for me. Therefore, you are to keep my Shabbat, because it is "Set apart" for you. Everyone who treats it as ordinary must be put to death; for whoever does any work on it is to be cut off from his people. On six days work will get done; but the seventh day is Shabbat, for complete rest, "Set apart" for YAHWEH Whoever does any work on the day of Shabbat must be put to death. The people of Yisra'el are to keep the Shabbat, to observe Shabbat through all their generations as a perpetual covenant. It is a sign between me and the people of Yisra'el forever; for in six days YAHWEH made heaven and earth, but on the seventh day he stopped working and rested.'"*

The text states that a person who does not honor the Sabbath is to be put to death. In this exile we are not to put anyone to death for violating any of the mitzvots that require the death penalty. However, in the mind of the Most High the person who does not honor the Sabbath is as though they don't exist to the Most High.

Purpose: The Sabbath is for creation to rest so that what YAHWEH created could be productive. The Sabbath gives man, also his creation, the opportunity to rest in order to be productive. Man is EL's creation.

The Commandment to Circumcise.

B'reshit (Gen) 17:9-13 *"EL said to Avraham, "As for you, you are to keep my covenant, you and your descendants after you, generation after generation. Here is my covenant, which you are to keep, between me and you, along with your descendants after* you: every male among you is to be circumcised. You are to be circumcised in the flesh of your foreskin; this will be the sign of the covenant between me and you. Generation after generation, **every male among you who is eight days old is to be circumcised**, including slaves born within your household and those bought from a foreigner not descended from you. The slave born in your house and the person bought with your money must be circumcised; thus my covenant will be in your flesh as an everlasting covenant. Any uncircumcised male who will not let himself be circumcised in the flesh of his foreskin—that person will be cut off from his people, because he has broken my covenant."

Purpose: YAHWEH wished to have a permanent symbol on the bodies of the Hebrew nation of Yisra'el to show that He set them apart from other nations. The Chosen people are perfected through the obligations of Torah. Therefore, the Most High left man the Torah to accomplish the completeness of his bodily form to man. This was so that it would be within man's ability and duty to also perfect the form of his soul by refining deeds. The removing of the foreskin around the penis needed to be accomplished as a permanent symbol. This procedure is to be done on the eighth day after the birth of all males. This applies everywhere we live in the land. It is the father's responsibility to have their sons circumcised and not the mother. This does not require a ritual ceremony by a Rabbis as is practiced by the Ashkenazi. It only requires that it is done. It may in this exile cost you extra to be done by your pediatrician.

The significance of this mitzvot takes us to Sh'mot 4:24 wherein Moshe almost lost his life for his failure to have his son's circumcised. The text, verse 24 *"At a lodging-place on the way, YAHWEH met Moshe and would have killed him, 25 had not Tzipporah taken a flintstone and cut off the foreskin of her son. She threw it at his feet, saying, "What a bloody bridegroom you are for me!" 26 But then, God let Moshe be. She added, "A bloody bridegroom because of the circumcision!"*

Prohibition to eat sinew.

B'reshit (Gen) 32:31 *"Ya'akov called the place P'ni-El [face of EL], "Because I have seen EL face to face, yet my life is spared." (31) As the sun rose upon him he went on past P'ni-El, limping at the hip. (32) This is why, to this day, the people of Yisra'el do not eat the thigh muscle that passes along the hip socket—because the man struck Ya'akov's hip at its socket."*

Purpose: This mitzvot is meant to be a reminder that as Ya'acov suffered at the hand of his brother Esau. In exile Hebrew Yisra'el will suffer many troubles in our various exiles at the hand of the nations. However, just as the sun set upon our father Ya'acov and he was healed so to the sun of redemption will one day set upon Hebrew Yisra'el and the nation will be healed and see its salvation.

This mitzvot applies everywhere the Hebrew people live throughout all generations. Sinew is to be removed from all meat. If we were koshering our own meat, then we would dig after it and remove it.

Prohibition to strike one's parents.

Sh'mot (Ex) 21:15-17 *"Whoever attacks his father or mother must be put to death. ... 17 "Whoever curses his father or mother must be put to death.*

Purpose: To enforce the necessary justice for the proper functioning of a civilized society. The hitting of one's parents under minds the very structure of the home which is supposed to be the primary building block of society. Therefore, it is a moral issue.

Compensation for injuring one's fellow man.

Sh'mot (Ex) 21:18,19 *"If two people fight, and one hits the other with a stone or with his fist, and the injured party doesn't die but is confined to his bed; 19 then, if he recovers enough to be able to walk around outside, even if with a cane, the attacker will be free of liability, except to compensate him for his loss of time and take responsibility for his care until his recovery is complete."*

Purpose: Is a matter of justice.

Prohibition against bestiality.

Sh'mot (Ex) 22:18 *"Whoever has sexual relations with an animal must be put to death."*

Purpose: To rid wickedness from the nation. While the penalty cannot be carried out in exile the act is wicked.

Prohibition to sacrifice to any god accept the Mighty One El.

Sh'mot (Ex) 22:19 *"Anyone who sacrifices to any god other than YAHWEH alone is to be completely destroyed."*

Purpose: To prevent idol worship. This penalty cannot be carried out in exile.

Prohibition to oppress a foreigner.

Sh'mot (Ex) 22:20 *"You must neither wrong nor oppress a foreigner living among you, for you yourselves were foreigners in the land of Egypt."*

Purpose: A foreigner (ger) is a person from the nations who converts and joins the Hebrew nations' way of faith. (Vayikra 19:33) 33 *"'If a foreigner stays with you in your land, do not do him wrong.*

Prohibition to abuse a widow or an orphan.

Sh'mot 22:21-23 *"You are not to abuse any widow or orphan. 22 If you do abuse them in any way, and they cry to me, I will certainly heed their cry. 23 My anger will burn, and I will kill you with the sword—your own wives will be widows and your own children fatherless."*

Purpose: This group of people does not have anyone to take up their cause; therefore, the Torah has enjoined us to acquire traits of kindness and mercy and be upright in all of our action towards them.

Obligation to lend money to the poor.

Sh'mot (Ex) 22:24 *"If you loan money to one of my people who is poor, you are not to deal with him as would a creditor; and you are not to charge him interest."*

Purpose: To show traits of kindness and compassion and to bestow goodness upon those of Hebrew Yisra'el who themselves are good. In particularly to those who are embarrassed by their need of having to beg. The words that follow are actions of a creditor.

Obligation not to collaborate in effecting an interest-based loan.

Sh'mot (Ex) 22:25,26 *"If you take your neighbor's coat as collateral, you are to restore it to him by sundown, 26 (27) because it is his only garment—he needs it to wrap his body; what else does he have in which to sleep? Moreover, if he cries out to me, I will listen; because I am compassionate."*

Purpose: To remove the pitfall of interest from the borrower's path. Thereby ensuring that one member of the nation of Yisra'el does not swallow up his fellow's resources without realizing his situation until he finds the borrower's home bereft of all goodness. This is the effect of interest.

Prohibition from cursing EL or a leader.

Sh'mot (Ex) 22:27 *""You are not to revile EL, and you are not to curse a leader of your people.*

Purpose: To revile means to be slight, swift, or trifling towards or blaspheming (by acting indifferent towards YAHWEH's mitzvots) or YAHWEH. Yisra'el is not to bring a curse upon a leader of the people as a means of intimidation in fair judgement.

Prohibition from eating Tereifah – torn flesh of an animal in the field.

Sh'mot (Ex) 22:30 *"You are to be my specially separated people. Therefore you are not to eat any flesh torn by wild animals in the countryside; rather, throw it out for the dogs."*

Purpose: The Torah distances us from anything that might cause impairment to our bodies, such as flesh of an animal or bird that has a fatal defect. It is to protect us from harmful effects of those foods.

Prohibition to listen to a false witness.

Sh'mot (Ex) 23:1 *"You are not to repeat false rumors; do not join hands with the wicked by offering perjured testimony."*

Purpose: To not judge or hear a claim of a person without the other being present. This also applies to a judge hearing one litigant without the presence of the other. This also applies to the text as is stated "do not repeat false rumors."

Prohibition to follow the crowd in any wrongdoing.

Sh'mot (Ex) 23:2 *"Do not follow the crowd when it does what is wrong; and don't allow the popular view to sway you into offering testimony for any cause if the effect will be to pervert justice."*

Purpose: We are commanded to emulate the Most High with deeds that attribute to him allowing our actions to be righteous.

The requirement not to have mercy upon a poor person in litigation just because he is poor.

Sh'mot (Ex) 23:3 *"On the other hand, don't favor a person's lawsuit simply because he is poor."*

Purpose: One is to judge fairly.

Prohibition to not defraud the innocent and the righteous.

Sh'mot (Ex) 23:7 *Keep away from fraud, and do not cause the death of the innocent and righteous; for I will not justify the wicked.*

Purpose: We are not to testify in a manner that would bring harm to the innocent or righteous that would cause them great harm unless you were a witness to what is being charged.

The obligation to relinquish ownership of all that the land produces in the seventh year.

Sh'mot (Ex) 23:10,11 *"For six years, you are to sow your land with seed and gather in its harvest. 11 But the seventh year, you are to let it rest and lie fallow, so that the poor among your people can eat; and what they leave, the wild animals in the countryside can eat. Do the same with your vineyard and olive grove."*

Purpose: To allow the land to rest and replenish itself; and for purposes stated in the text. This applies to those in this exile who raise crops.

Obligation to rest on *the Sabbath.*

Sh'mot (Ex) 23:12 "For six days, you are to work. But on the seventh day, you are to rest, so that your ox and donkey can rest, and your slave-girl's son and the foreigner be renewed."

Purpose: While text speaks of the animals in this exile it speaks to anything and/or person that is used to produce work.

It is to rest on the Sabbath so that its strength can be renewed.

When does the Sabbath begin and end? In order to understand this, you can't think Gregorian in that a new day starts at 12:01am. This is still darkness and not a new day in the mind of the creator. According to text in B'reshit 1, there are three aspects to defining a day "*4 God saw that the light was good, and God divided the light from the darkness. 5 God called the light Day, and the darkness he called Night. So there was evening, and there was morning, one day.* Here is how it works. Firstly, El called the light day; secondly, El called the darkness night; and thirdly El called the morning day. So, day does not start until the sun breaks the horizon in the east. This is when the Sabbath begins. Sabbath is until the sun goes down and evening begins trending towards darkness as light has ended.

Obligation to pay attention to what YAHWEH says.

Sh'mot (Ex) 23:13 *"Pay attention to everything I have said to you; do not invoke the names of other gods or even let them be heard crossing your lips."*

Purpose: The question should always be, what did YAHWEH say? This purpose is also about subverting Hebrew Yisra'el from idolatry. It is the Hebrew nations need to always lean and pay attention to what EL says and what he says to his prophets.

Prohibition to anoint a person's body with the Anointing Oil.

Sh'mot (Ex) 30:31-33 *"Tell the people of Yisra'el, 'This is to be a holy anointing oil for me through all your generations. 32 It is not to be used for anointing a person's body; and you are not to make any like it, with the same composition of ingredients—it is holy, and you are to treat it as holy. 33 Whoever makes any like it or uses it on any unauthorized person is to be cut off from his people.'"*

Purpose: It is improper for common folk to use this exalted oil that is housed in the Temple. The Anointing Oil use is for only the choicest of the nation of Yisra'el, the Cohanim, Kings, and the set apart articles. By depriving this oil from the common, it remains most precious in the eyes of Hebrew Yisra'el as it is germane to the Temple, and its set apart use. It has been common practice for the laying on of hands with anointing oil on people. This comes from the Greek text which says in Luke 7:46, You didn't put oil on my head, but this woman poured perfume on my feet! Also, James 5:14 Is someone among you ill? He should call for the elders of the congregation. They will pray for him and rub olive oil on him in the name of the Lord. The prayer offered with trust will heal the one who is ill—the Lord will restore his health; and if he has committed sins, he will be forgiven. The mitzvot stated by Moshe given to him by the Most High holds precedence over the Greek text. The EL of Hebrew Yisra'el says don't do it.

Prohibition to replicate the incense.

Sh'mot (Ex) 30:34-37 *"YAHWEH said to Moshe, "Take aromatic plant substances—balsam resin, sweet onycha root and bitter galbanum gum—these spices along with frankincense, all in equal quantities; 35 and make incense, blended and perfumed as would an expert perfume-maker, salted, pure and holy. 36 You are to grind up some of it very finely and put it in front of the testimony in the tent of meeting where I will meet with you; you are to regard it as especially holy. 37 You are not to make for your own use any incense like it, with the same composition of ingredients—you are to treat it as holy, for YAHWEH. 38 Whoever makes up any like it to use as perfume is to be cut off from his people."*

Purpose: This is a special incense that is reserved only for the Temple in the Land of Hebrew Yisra'el and grandeur of the Temple and all that is in it in the people's eyes. This mitzvot is germane to the ingredients listed and not incense in general.

Obligation to keep the Sabbath.

Sh'mot (Ex) 31:12 *YAHWEH said to Moshe, 13 "Tell the people of Yisra'el, 'You are to observe my Shabbats; for this is a sign between me and you through all your generations; so that you will know that I am YAHWEH, who sets you apart for me. 14 Therefore you are to keep my Shabbat, because it is Set apart for you. Everyone who treats it as ordinary must be put to death; for whoever does any work on it is to be cut off from his people. 15 On six days work will get done; but the seventh day is Shabbat, for complete rest, Set apart for YAHWEH. Whoever does any work on the day of Shabbat must be put to death. 16 The people of Yisra'el are to keep the Shabbat, to observe Shabbat through all their generations as a perpetual covenant. 17 It is a sign between me and the people of Yisra'el forever; for in six days YAHWEH made heaven and earth, but on the seventh day he stopped working and rested.'"*

Purpose: Is the same as stated in B'reshit (Gen) 2:1-3. Accept in this commandment the Most High deems it as being a sign between us and him forever and that it is a set apart day. He defines what we are supposed to do and how he feels about our not being obedient to his request. For Hebrew Yisra'el one's failure to keep the Shabbat to the Most High is an act of wickedness.

Historical study and statements from the Catholic Church acknowledge that the Greeks and the Romans changed the 7th day Sabbath, that the Most High ordained, to the 1st day of the week Sunday just because they could and wanted to and not by any direction from El.

Prohibition to consume idolatrous worship.

Sh'mot (Ex) 34:12,14 *Be careful not to make a covenant with the people living in the land where you are going, so that they won't become a snare within your own borders. . . . 14 because you are not to bow down to any other god; since YAHWEH—whose very name is Jealous—is a jealous EL.*

Purpose: To prevent idolatry from being a part of the Hebrew nation and to prevent wickedness.

Prohibition to kindle a fire on the Shabbat.

Sh'mot (Ex) 35:3 *You are not to kindle a fire in any of your homes on Shabbat."*

Purpose: Is to glorify this day so that it should be a day of rest. As far as cooking is concerned, cooking is permitted until the sun breaks the horizon on the seventh day. After that we are commanded not to kindle a fire. If something is already cooked. It can be heated as it is already created. Kindling a fire is related to doing that which creates.

Chapter Summary/Key Takeaways

TEHILLIM (PSALMS 119:33-35 *Teach me, YAHWEH, the way of your laws; keeping them will be its own reward for me. 34 Give me understanding; then I will keep your Torah I will observe it with all my heart. 35 Guide me on the path of your mitzvot, for I take pleasure in it.*

NOTES:

CHAPTER THREE

APPLICABLE TORAH MITZVAHS VAYIKRA (LEV)

Prohibition to eat fat or blood.

Vayikra (Lev) 3:17 *It is to be a permanent regulation through all your generations wherever you live that you will eat neither fat nor blood.'"* 19:26 *"'Do not eat anything with blood."*

Purpose: Fat is suitable for burning for fuel. Fat is thick and hard to digest. While the soul is in the blood. The effect of eating blood causes man to assimilate himself with the animal's life force, thereby diluting the spiritual quality of his own soul. There should be no reference to eating or drinking blood.

In the book of John, Jesus says, 6:55 For my flesh is true food, and my blood is true drink. Whoever eats my flesh and drinks my blood lives in me, and I live in him. And in 1Corinthians Paul writes 11:25 "This cup is the New Covenant effected by my blood; do this, as often as you drink it, as a memorial to me." How does this fit with what the Most High says. Remember the mitzvot in Sh'mot (Ex) 23:13 *"Pay attention to everything I have said to you.* Drinking blood and eating someone's body even as a suggested metaphor violates this mitzvot. Whose right Jesus or the Creator, the Set Apart Spirit El?

Anybody who knows evidence must testify in court.

Vayikra (Lev) 5:1 *"If a person who is a witness, sworn to testify, sins by refusing to tell what he has seen or heard about the matter, he must bear the consequences."*

Purpose: This is pertinent in order to purge evil and distance people from sin.

Prohibition to consume blood of any animal.

Vayikra 7:26,27 *"You are not to eat any kind of blood, whether from birds or animals, in any of your homes. 27 Whoever eats any blood will be cut off from his people.'"* Vayikra 17:10-12 *"When someone from the community of Yisra'el or one of the foreigners living with you eats any kind of blood, I will set myself against that person who eats blood and cut him off from his people. 11 For the life of a creature is in the blood, and I have given it to you on the altar to make atonement for yourselves; for it is the blood that makes atonement because of the life.' 12 This is why I told the people of Yisra'el, 'None of you is to eat blood, nor is any foreigner living with you to eat blood.'"*

Purpose: This has the same purpose as in Vayikra (Lev) 3:17 above. In this mitzvot the Most High states his reason saying that "life, is in the blood."

Hebrew Dietary Prohibitions

As we talk about the dietary laws in some people's mind what comes to thought is 1 Timothy 4:3 *They forbid marriage and require abstinence from foods which El created to be eaten with thanksgiving by those who have come to trust and to know the truth. 4 For everything created by El is good, and nothing received with thanksgiving needs to be rejected, 5 because the word of El and prayer make it holy.* Don't allow this Greek text to confuse you. Remember who Timothy is and what his testimony is from Sha'ul. He is a Hebrew and familiar with Torah Law. In this text he is speaking to Hebrews, so he and they know what is considered to food according to Vayikra (Lev) Chapter 11. This text is misleading as many of the Greek text are when it comes to validation against the foundation, the set apart Scriptures. Everything while being made good is not good as food to be consumed by human beings. A note to remember people of the nations can do whatever they want to do however, if you call yourself a pure Hebrew Yisra'lite then it is incumbent upon you to know what food is and what is not according to Torah Law. The Most High El is very specific.

Not to eat non-kosher animals.

Vayikra (Lev) 11:4-7 *"But you are not to eat those that only chew the cud or only have a separate hoof. For example, the camel, the coney and the hare are unclean for you, because they chew the cud but don't have a separate hoof; 7 while the pig is unclean for you, because, although it has a separate and completely divided hoof, it doesn't chew the cud."*

Purpose: They are detestable or an abomination to the Most High as they are unclean and are not considered to be food by the Most High EL.

To examine the scales of fish to distinguish between kosher and non-kosher.

Vayikra (Lev) 11: 9 *"'Of all the things that live in the water, you may eat these: anything in the water that has fins and scales, whether in seas or in rivers—these you may eat."*

Purpose: These sea, river, or ocean fish are clean by the standards of the Most High and are eatable.

Prohibition to eat non-kosher fish.

Vayikra 11:10-12 *"But everything in the seas and rivers without both fins and scales, of all the small water-creatures and of all the living creatures in the water, is a detestable thing for you. 11 Yes, these will be detestable for you—you are not to eat their meat, and you are to detest their carcasses. 12 Whatever lacks fins and scales in the water is a detestable thing for you."*

Purpose: These are unclean, are not food and should not be eaten by Hebrew Yisra'el. These creatures were for the purpose of cleaning the eco system. They eat dung and other filth in the waters. Just to name a few these include shrimp, crab, lobster, clams, calamari, and crawdads.

Vayikra 11:13- 20 Non-kosher birds.

Vayikra (Lev) 11: 13-20 *"'The following creatures of the air are to be detestable for you—they are not to be eaten, they are a detestable thing: the eagle, the vulture, the osprey, 14 the kite, the various kinds of buzzards, 15 the various kinds of ravens, 16 the ostrich, the screech-owl, the seagull, the various kinds of hawks, 17 the little owl, the cormorant, the great owl, 18 the horned owl, the pelican, the barn owl, 19 the stork, the various kinds of herons, the hoopoe and the bat. 20 "'All winged swarming creatures that go on all fours are a detestable thing for you."*

Purpose: These birds are unclean. They clean the land, eating that which is call filth. The Most High deems them detestable or an abomination.

To examine the signs of locusts to distinguish between kosher and non-kosher.

Vayikra (Lev) 11:20-23 *"All winged swarming creatures that go on all fours are a detestable thing for you; 21 except that of all winged swarming creatures that go on all fours, you may eat those that have jointed legs above their feet, enabling them to jump off the ground. 22 Specifically, of these you may eat the various kinds of locusts, grasshoppers, katydids and crickets. 23 But other than that, all winged swarming creatures having four feet are a detestable thing for you."*

Purpose: To distinguish between those creatures that are clean and those that are not; filth vs. those that are eatable.

The mitzvot gives us the understanding of what to look for when distinguishing what is eatable.

Not to eat non-kosher creatures that crawl on land.

Vayikra (Lev) 11:41- 45 *"'Any creature that swarms on the ground is a detestable thing; it is not to be eaten- 42 whatever moves on its stomach, goes on all fours, or has many legs—all creatures that swarm on the ground; you are not to eat them, because they are a detestable thing. 43 You are not to make yourselves detestable with any of these swarming, crawling creatures; do not make yourselves unclean with them, do not defile yourselves with them. 44 For I am YAHWEH your EL; therefore, consecrate yourselves and be set apart, for I am Set apart; and do not defile yourselves with any kind of swarming creature that moves along the ground. (Maftir) 45 For I am YAHWEH, who brought you up out of the land of Egypt to be your EL. Therefore you are to be set apart, because I am set apart."*

Purpose: To keep our bodies clean in the eyes of the Most High. The Most High tells us what is detestable or an abomination to him meaning he hates these things. Why, because they are a detriment to our bodies.

Laws governing impurity and sexual relationships

Observe the laws of impurity caused by childbirth.

Vayikra (Lev) 12:2-5 *"Tell the people of Yisra'el: 'If a woman conceives and gives birth to a boy, she will be unclean for seven days with the same uncleanness as in niddah, when she is having her menstrual period. 5 But if she gives birth to a girl, she will be unclean for two weeks, as in her niddah; and she is to wait another sixty-six days to be purified from her blood."*

Purpose: Is for the purpose of establishing a time frame for the healing of the woman who during childbirth maintains an excess of blood within her body which cause her to not be completely healed. This mitzvot is established for medical reasons.

Obligation to circumcise all males on the eighth day after birth.

Vayikra (Lev) 12:3 *"On the eighth day, the baby's foreskin is to be circumcised."*

Purpose: See explanation in B'reshit 17:9-13. This is a requirement for every male child. It is the blood covenant. It is necessary for a male to be circumcised in his flesh in order to participate in Pesach Sh'mote (Exo)12:43 43 *YAHWEH said to Moshe and Aharon, "This is the regulation for the Pesach lamb: no foreigner is to eat it. 44 But if anyone has a slave he bought for money, when you have circumcised him, he may eat it.*

Observe the laws of impurity of a seminal emission (regular ejaculation with normal semen).

Vayikra (Lev)15:16,17 *"If a man has a seminal emission, he is to bathe his entire body in water; he will be unclean until evening. 17 Any clothing or leather on which there is any semen is to be washed with water; it will be unclean until evening."*

Purpose: To maintain purity and cleanliness. This act occurs when a man has thoughts regarding bodily desires. Thusly the body is deemed impure through these desires. By washing it is the purpose for man to cleanse himself of such thoughts.

Obligation to bathe after sexual relations.

Vayikra 15:18 "If a man goes to bed with a woman and has sexual relations, both are to bathe themselves in water; they will be unclean until evening."

Purpose: To maintain cleanline.

Observe the laws of menstrual impurity.

Vayikra (Lev) 15:19,20, *"If a woman has a discharge, and the discharge from her body is blood, she will be in her state of niddah for seven days. Whoever touches her will be unclean until evening. 20 Everything she lies on or sits on in her state of niddah will be unclean.*

Purpose: Parts of this mitzvot, at this time of our exile, is more germane to the Temple in the land. Since we do not have the Temple and we are in exile we are all presumed to be contaminated by coming in contact with things that would make us unclean. The only practical application to this mitzvot is relative to marital relations. The woman in niddah is not to engage in marital relations as long as she is in niddah. She is unclean; therefore, in order to maintain purity and cleanliness this mitzvot is in play as stated.

Observe the laws of impurity caused by a woman's running issue.

Vayikra (Lev) 15:25 *"If a woman has a discharge of blood for many days not during her period, or if her discharge lasts beyond the normal end of her period, then throughout the time she is having an unclean discharge she will be as when she is in niddah—she is unclean."*

Purpose: Is the same as above with this exception. The fact that her flow is longer than usual can be very harmful and especially to anyone who cohabits with her.

Prohibition to engage in activities of the nations that violate YAHWEH's Mitzvots.

Vayikra (Lev) 18:2 *"Speak to the people of Yisra'el; tell them, 'I am YAHWEH your EL. 3 You are not to engage in the activities found in the land of Egypt, where you used to live; and you are not to engage in the activities found in the land of Kena'an, where I am bringing you; nor are you to live by their laws."*

Purpose: This mitzvot speaks to practices which are contrary to the Hebrew way of life that violates any one of YAHWEH's mitzvots. It makes common sense that this mitzvot also applies to this exile. While the text speaks of Egypt and Kena'an the intent of the commandment is germane to anywhere in the world Hebrew Yisra'el lives at all times.

Obligation to obey YAHWEH's rulings and laws.

Vayikra (Lev) 18:4 *"You are to obey my rulings and laws and live accordingly; I am YAHWEH your EL 5 You are to observe my laws and rulings; if a person does them, he will have life through them; I am YAHWEH."*

Purpose: It is obvious that our responsibility is to obey the Most High. This commandment is relative to the prior one.

Prohibition to have sexual relations with a relative.

Vayikra 18:6 *"'None of you is to approach anyone who is a close relative in order to have sexual relations; I am YAHWEH.*

Purpose: We are forbidden to act intimately in any manner with a relative. This is to protect the morality of the Hebrew nation. This mitzvot is moral and ethical. This mitzvot is parallel to D'varim (Deu) 27:16-23 16 *"'A curse on anyone who dishonors his father or mother.' All the people are to say, 'Amen!' 17 "'A curse on anyone who moves his neighbor's boundary marker.' All the people are to say, 'Amen!' 18 "'A curse on anyone who causes a blind person to lose his way on the road.' All the people are to say, 'Amen!' 19 "'A curse on anyone who interferes with justice for the foreigner, orphan or widow.' All the people are to say, 'Amen!' 20 "'A curse on anyone who has sexual relations with his father's wife, because he has violated his father's rights.' All the people are to say, 'Amen!' 21 "'A curse on anyone who has sexual relations with any kind of animal.' All the people are to say, 'Amen!' 22 "'A curse on* *anyone who has sexual relations with his sister, no matter whether she is the daughter of his father or of his mother.' All the people are to say, 'Amen!' 23 "'A curse on anyone who has sexual relations with his mother-in-law.' All the people are to say, 'Amen!'*

Prohibition not to have sexual relations with your father or mother.

Vayikra (Lev) 18:7,8 *"You are not to have sexual relations with your father, and you are not to have sexual relations with your mother. She is your mother—do not have sexual relations with her. 8 You are not to have sexual relations with your father's wife; that is your father's prerogative."*

Purpose: We are forbidden to act intimately in a manner with a relative. This is to protect the morality of the Hebrew nation. This mitzvot is moral and ethical.

Not to have sexual relations with your sister.

Vayikra (Lev) 18:9 *"You are not to have sexual relations with your sister, the daughter of your father or the daughter of your mother, whether born at home or elsewhere. Do not have sexual relations with them.:*

Purpose: We are forbidden to act intimately in any manner with a relative. This is to protect the morality of the Hebrew nation. This mitzvot is moral and ethical.

Not to have sexual relations with your son's daughter.

Vayikra (Lev) 18:10 *"You are not to have sexual relations with your son's daughter or with your daughter's daughter. Do not have sexual relations with them, because their sexual disgrace will be your own."*

Purpose: We are forbidden to act intimately in any manner with a relative. This is to protect the morality of the Hebrew nation. This mitzvot is moral and ethical.

Not to have sexual relations with your daughter's daughter.

Vayikra (Lev) 18:10 *"You are not to have sexual relations with your son's daughter or with your daughter's daughter. Do not have sexual relations with them, because their sexual disgrace will be your own."*

Purpose: We are forbidden to act intimately in any manner with a relative. This is to protect the morality of the Hebrew nation. This mitzvot is moral and ethical.

Not to have sexual relations with your father's wife's daughter.

Vayikra (Lev) 18:11 *"You are not to have sexual relations with your father's wife's daughter, born to your father, because she is your sister; do not have sexual relations with her."*

Purpose: We are forbidden to act intimately in any manner with a relative. This is to protect the morality of the Hebrew nation. This mitzvot is moral and ethical.

Not to have sexual relations with your father's sister.

Vayikra (Lev) 18:12 *"You are not to have sexual relations with your father's sister, because she is your father's close relative."*

Purpose: We are forbidden to act intimately in any manner with a relative. This is to protect the morality of the Hebrew nation. This mitzvot is moral and ethical.

Not to have sexual relations with your mother's sister.

Vayikra (Lev) 18:13 *"You are not to have sexual relations with your mother's sister, because she is your mother's close relative."*

Purpose: We are forbidden to act intimately in any manner with a relative. This is to protect the morality of the Hebrew nation. This mitzvot is moral and ethical.

Not to have sexual relations with your father's brother's wife.

Vayikra (Lev) 18:14 *"You are not to disgrace your father's brother by having sexual relations with his wife, because she is your aunt."*

Purpose: We are forbidden to act intimately in any manner with a relative. This is to protect the morality of the Hebrew nation. This mitzvot is moral and ethical.

Not to have sexual relations with your son's wife.

Vayikra (Lev) 18:15 *"You are not to have sexual relations with your daughter-in-law, because she is your son's wife. Do not have sexual relations with her."*

Purpose: We are forbidden to act intimately in any manner with a relative. This is to protect the morality of the Hebrew nation. This mitzvot is moral and ethical.

Not to have sexual relations with your brother's wife.

Vayikra (Lev) 18:16 *"You are not to have sexual relations with your brother's wife, because this is your brother's prerogative."*

Purpose: We are forbidden to act intimately in any manner with a relative. This is to protect the morality of the Hebrew nation. This mitzvot is moral and ethical.

Not to have sexual relations with a woman and her daughter, nor her son's daughter, nor her daughter's daughter.

Vayikra (Lev) 18:17 *"You are not to have sexual relations with both a woman and her daughter, nor are you to have sexual relations with her son's daughter or her daughter's daughter; they are close relatives of hers, and it would be shameful."*

Purpose: We are forbidden to act intimately in any manner with a relative. This is to protect the morality of the Hebrew nation. This mitzvot is moral and ethical.

Not to have sexual relations with your wife's sister.

Vayikra (Lev) 18:18 *"You are not to take a woman to be a rival with her sister and have sexual relations with her while her sister is still alive."*

Purpose: We are forbidden to act intimately in any manner with a relative. This is to protect the morality of the Hebrew nation. This mitzvot is moral and ethical.

Not to have sexual relations with a menstrual impure woman.

Vayikra (Lev) 18:19 *"You are not to approach a woman in order to have sexual relations with her when she is unclean from her time of niddah."*

Purpose: We are forbidden to act intimately in any manner with a woman when she is impure (unclean) during her menstrual cycle. This is to protect the morality of the Hebrew nation. This mitzvot is moral and ethical.

Not to have sexual relations with someone else's wife.

Vayikra (Lev)18:20 *"You are not to go to bed with your neighbor's wife and thus become unclean with her."*

Purpose: We are forbidden to act intimately in any manner with another man's wife. This is to protect the morality of the Hebrew nation. This mitzvot is moral and ethical.

Not to have homosexual sexual relations.

Vayikra (Lev) 18:22 *"You are not to go to bed with a man as with a woman; it is an abomination.*

Purpose: We are forbidden to act intimately in any manner with members of the same sex. This is to protect the morality of the Hebrew nation. This mitzvot is moral and ethical.

A man must not have sexual relations with a beast

Vayikra (Lev) 18:23 *"You are not to have sexual relations with any kind of animal and thus become unclean with it"*

Purpose: We are forbidden to act intimately in any manner with animals. This is to protect the morality of the Hebrew nation. This mitzvot is moral and ethical.

Prohibition of bestiality for a woman.

Vayikra (Lev) 18:23 *"nor is any woman to present herself to an animal to have sexual relations with it; it is perversion."*

Purpose: We are forbidden to have sexual relations with an animal. This mitzvot speaks to morality.

These are the Mitzvahs concerning being Set Apart

Vayikra 19:1 *YAHWEH said to Moshe, 2 "Speak to the entire community of Yisra'el; tell them, 'You people are to be set-apart because I, YAHWEH your EL, am set-apart.*

The obligation to revere one's father and mother.

Vayikra (Lev) 19:3 *"Every one of you is to revere his father and mother, and you are to keep my Shabbats; I am YAHWEH your EL."*

Purpose: This is a moral and ethical mitzvot. Also, it is necessary to recognize and to bestow kindness to those who have been kind to you and not treat one's parents as though they are strangers.

Not to inquire into idolatry/Not to make an idol for others.

Vayikra (Lev) 19:4 *"Do not turn to idols, and do not cast metal gods for yourselves; I am YAHWEH your EL."*

Purpose: Hebrew Yisra'el is to distance from all aspects of idolatry

Prohibition to steal anything.

Vayikra (Lev) 19:11 *"Do not steal from, defraud, or lie to each other."*

Purpose: This is a moral and ethical mitzvot. It is to keep wickedness from the nation and is a matter of common sense.

Do not swear by the Most High's name falsely.

Vayikra (Lev) 19:12 *"Do not swear by my name falsely, which would be profaning the name of your EL; I am YAHWEH."*

Purpose: This mitzvot prohibits a person from swearing by the name of El mischievously. This mitzvot relates to a person making oaths of utterances within one's own ability to do or not to do something and invoking the Most High into it.

Not to rob openly/Not to withhold wages or fail to repay a debt.

Vayikra (Lev) 19 13 *"Do not oppress or rob your neighbor; specifically, you are not to keep back the wages of a hired worker all night until morning."*

Purpose: This mitzvot is germane to morality and ethical behavior. The nation of Yisra'el is admonished not to withhold a worker's wages. The reason being is that the worker needs his earnings to care for his family.

Not to put a stumbling block before a blind man (nor give harmful advice).

Vayikra (Lev) 19:14 *"Do not speak a curse against a deaf person or place an obstacle in the way of a blind person; rather, fear your El; I am YAHWEH."*

Purpose: Both of these two categories, deaf and blind, speak to people who are devoid of knowledge and lacking understanding. It also, relates to not placing a curse upon a person saying that it would be a detriment to his or her life. Putting a stumbling block before a blind person speaks to misleading a person seeking truth.

The prohibition to pervert justice.

Vayikra (Lev) 19:15 *"'Do not be unjust in judging—show neither partiality to the poor nor deference to the mighty, but with justice judge your neighbor.*

Purpose: This mitzvot is moral and ethical.

The prohibition of spreading gossip.

Vayikra (Lev) 19:16 *"Do not go around spreading slander among your people, but also don't stand idly by when your neighbor's life is at stake; I am YAHWEH."*

Purpose: This mitzvot is moral and ethical. Gossip is cause for quarrel and strife and can lead to bloodshed. The Most High El desires good from Hebrew Yisra'el and commanded us concerning, *Lashon hara,* disparaging speech that conveys something negative. And *rechilus* which is simply the conveying of information that has the ability to cause the listener resentment towards a person.

Prohibition to stand idle while ones fellow Hebrew is in danger.

Vayikra (Lev) 19:16 *"but also don't stand idly by when your neighbor's life is at stake; I am YAHWEH.*

Purpose: This mitzvot is moral and ethical. Just as one will save his fellow man when he is in danger, so will his fellowman save him when he is in danger. It also protects humankind and the habitation of the world. Yeshayahu 45:*18 For thus says YAHWEH, who created the heavens, EL, who shaped and made the earth, who established and created it not to be chaos, but formed it to be lived in: "I am YAHWEH; there is no other.*

Prohibition to hate your fellow Hebrew.

Vayikra (Lev) 19:17,18 *"Do not hate your brother in your heart, but rebuke your neighbor frankly, so that you won't carry sin because of him. 18 Don't take vengeance on or bear a grudge against any of your people; rather, love your neighbor as yourself; I am YAHWEH."*

Purpose: This mitzvot is both moral, ethical, and relative to treating our fellow man rightly. You reap what you sow.

Obligation to observe YAHWEH's regulations. The prohibition to mate animals of different species. The prohibition to wear a garment made of two different kinds of thread.

Vayikra (Lev) 19:19 *" 19 "Observe my regulations. "Don't let your livestock mate with those of another kind, don't sow your field with two different kinds of grain, and don't wear a garment of cloth made with two different kinds of thread.*

Purpose: This is what the Most High ask of his people throughout all generations so that they may live. He asks us to *Observe my regulations.* This text is specific to creation. All that the Most High created he deemed to be perfect and good.

When man augments what the Most High has deemed perfect and good it now becomes imperfect, less than its intended purpose. In the long run many things that become augmented can be harmful to man's health or a detriment to one's life. It also says that what the Most High made was not perfect and good. Everything the Most High El created has purpose. The efficiency of the Most High EL says do not mix two kinds of garments. Mixing wool and linen with other fibers destroys the effectiveness of the pure fibers of wool that keeps you warm as does linen that keeps you cool.

Prohibition to practice divination or fortune-telling.

Vayikra (Lev)19:26 *"Do not practice divination or fortune-telling. D'varim 18:9 "When you enter the land YAHWEH your EL is giving you, you are not to learn how to follow the abominable practices of those nations. 10 There must not be found among you anyone who makes his son or daughter pass through fire, a diviner, a soothsayer, an enchanter, a sorcerer, 11 a spell-caster, a consulter of ghosts or spirits, or a necromancer. 12 For whoever does these things is detestable to YAHWEH, and because of these abominations YAHWEH your EL is driving them out ahead of you. 13 You must be wholehearted with YAHWEH your EL. (v) 14 For these nations, which you are about to dispossess, listen to soothsayers and diviners; but you, YAHWEH your EL does not allow you to do this."*

Purpose: Is stated within the text and is germane to practices of idolatry. The application of this text is anywhere Hebrew Yisra'el lives.

Prohibition to etch a tattoo upon our flesh.

Vayikra (Lev) 19:28 28 *"Don't cut gashes in your flesh when someone dies or tattoo yourselves; I am YAHWEH."*

Purpose: We are to distance ourselves from all manner

of idolatry from our bodies and from our consciences. This practice was custom to idolaters to mark themselves for their deity with tattoos. This practice should not be common amongst YAHWEH'S people.

Prohibition to debase your daughter.

Vayikra (Lev) 19:29 *"Do not debase your daughter by making her a prostitute, so that the land will not fall into prostitution and become full of shame."*

Purpose: As stated within the text do not lower the reputation or devalue your daughter. In the aspect of land, it refers to ones dwelling place. Don't defile your home by doing that which is wicked.

Obligation to keep the Shabbats.

Vayikra (Lev) 19:30 *"Keep my Shabbats and revere my sanctuary; I am YAHWEH."*

Purpose: Is stated in B'reshit 2:1-3.

Prohibition to curse one's father or mother.

Vayikra (Lev) 20:9 *"A person who curses his father or mother must be put to death; having cursed his father or his mother, his blood is on him."*

Purpose: The primary Torah obligation is to teach the things that are germane to moral conduct. One of which is respecting one's parents. We are to show them reverence; they are the ones who brought you into this world. The issue is not whether they were good or bad parents we are commanded to show them respect.

Prohibition for the Cohanim to marry a prostitute.

Vayikra (Lev) 21:7 *"A cohen is not to marry a woman who*

is a prostitute, who has been profaned or who has been divorced; because he is set apart for his EL. Rather, you are to set him apart as set apart, because he offers the bread of your EL; he is to be Set apart for you, because I, YAHWEH, who makes you Set apart, am Set apart.

Purpose: Torah verbiage does not use Christian terminology relegated to leaders or overseers such as pastor. The leader of the congregation is a Cohanim which means priest/teacher. While we do not have cohanim from the linage of Aharon in this exile, the congregational leader functions in that office. Therefore, this mitzvot is applicable. The Hebrew congregational leader must be set apart and follow the rule of this mitzvot.

The obligation for the Cohanim to marry a virgin.

Vayikra (Lev) 21:13 *"He is to marry a virgin; 14 he may not marry a widow, divorcee, profaned woman or prostitute; but he must marry a virgin from among his own people 15 and not disqualify his descendants among his people; because I am YAHWEH, who makes him set apart."*

Purpose: As stated above.

Obligation to not profane YAHWEH's name.

Vayikra (Lev) 22:32 *You are not to profane my holy name; on the contrary, I am to be regarded as holy among the people of Yisra'el.*

Purpose: Is not to desecrate the name of the Most High by any means at all. Especially by ones conduct and actions we are to hold his name high and respectful by our actions. Ezekiel 20: 39 *"As for you, house of Yisra'el, here is what YAHWEH ELOHIM says: 'Go on serving your idols, every one of you! But afterwards, [I swear that] you will listen to me, and you will no longer profane my holy name with your gifts and with your idols.*

Mitzvahs relating to the Moedims (Festivals of YAHWEH) which are High Sabbaths

Obligation to keep the Sabbath.

Vayikra (Lev) 23:3 *"Work is to be done on six days; but the seventh day is a Shabbat of complete rest, a holy convocation; you are not to do any kind of work; it is a Shabbat for YAHWEH, even in your homes."*

Purpose: Previously stated in Sh'mot (Ex) 31

Obligation to rest on the first day of Pesach.

Vayikra (Lev) 23:4-7 *"'These are the designated times of YAHWEH, the holy convocations you are to proclaim at their designated times. 5 "In the first month, on the fourteenth day of the month, between sundown and complete darkness, comes Pesach for YAHWEH. 7 On the first day you are to have a holy convocation; don't do any kind of ordinary work."*

Purpose: We should reflect upon the significance of this festival. It is a time of remembrance of how YAHWEH brought our ancestors out of the abode of slavery to be free men. We were never supposed to be enslaved again. But by not following and obeying the Most High, history chronicles our fate.

Obligation to eat matzah for seven days and have a holy convocation/do no ordinary work.

Vayikra (Lev) 23:6-8 *"On the fifteenth day of the same month is the festival of matzah; for seven days you are to eat matzah. 7 On the first day you are to have a holy convocation; don't do any kind of ordinary work. 8 Bring an offering made by fire to YAHWEH for seven days. On the seventh day is a holy convocation; do not do any kind of ordinary work.'"*

Purpose: This is a time of remembrance of when our

ancestors left Mitzrayim (Egypt) in a hurry and did not have time for their bread to rise. It is also indicative of the removing of leaven which represents haughtiness. This is a *set apart* time to YAHWEH. Bringing an offering made of fire. If we were in the land this would be an animal or an offering that could go up in smoke. In this exile we offer a monetary offering. As D'varim (Deu) 16:16 says *"They are not to show up before YAHWEH empty-handed, 17 but every man is to give what he can, in accordance with the blessing YAHWEH your EL has given you.*

Obligation to count the Omer.

Vayikra (Lev) 23:15,16 *"From the day after the day of rest—that is, from the day you bring the sheaf for waving—you are to count seven full weeks, 16 until the day after the seventh week; you are to count fifty days; and then you are to present a new grain offering to YAHWEH."*

Purpose: The simple purpose is to focus on the time in which YAHWEH gave to the Hebrew nation the Torah and to celebrate.

Obligation to bring bread of wheat from our homes on Shavuot.

Vayikra (Lev) 23:17 *"You must bring bread from your homes for waving—two loaves made with one gallon of fine flour, baked with leaven—as first fruits for YAHWEH."*

Purpose: The significant reason for bringing the loaves of bread is to acknowledge the kindness of YAHWEH. The loaves of bread are a form of thanksgiving to YAHWEH for the new harvest. We do not have a wheat harvest in exile unless you are a wheat farmer. The bringing of the bread is a symbolic act for persons who are not wheat farmers; it demonstrates our thanksgiving to the Most High EL.

Obligation to rest and do no ordinary work on the Festival of Shavuot.

Vayikra (Lev) 23:21 *"On the same day, you are to call a set apart convocation; do not do any kind of ordinary work; this is a permanent regulation through all your generations, no matter where you live."*

Purpose: This festival according to Scripture occurs in the third month and the eleventh day. It is strictly the celebration of the Spring harvest. This will always be on a Sabbath usually in May. This date for Shavuot does not follow the Ashkenaz calendar but the Most High's calendar based on Scripture text. Order your calendar: www.hebraiccalendar.com

Obligation to rest on the day of Feast of Trumpets.

Vayikra (Lev) 23:24 *"YAHWEH said to Moshe, 24 "Tell the people of Yisra'el, 'In the seventh month, the first of the month is to be for you a day of complete rest for remembering, a set apart convocation announced with blasts on the shofar."*

Purpose: The sound of the Trumpets/Shofar is for the purpose of awakening Hebrew Yisra'el to the seriousness of the day and the days ahead in particularly the Day of Atonement.

Obligation to fast and *bring an offering made of fire on the day of Atonement.*

Vayikra (Lev) 23:26, 27 *YAHWEH said to Moshe, 27 "The tenth day of this seventh month is Yom-Kippur; you are to have a set apart convocation, you are to deny yourselves, and you are to bring an offering made by fire to YAHWEH.*

Purpose: There are three parts to this mitzvot (1) have a set apart convocation, (2) deny ourselves, and (3) bring an offering. The first is the convocation. We are to gather and fellowship. This is the finale day to teshuvah (repent) and start a new season of life. Second denying ourselves for these 24 hours is about cleansing our inner parts as well as arriving at a better spiritual place in our lives. Third is to bring an offering. In the land this would be an animal. In this exile it's money.

Prohibition to do any kind of ordinary work on the Day of Atonement.

Vayikra (Lev) 23:28, 32 *You are not to do any kind of work on that day, because it is Yom-Kippur, to make atonement for you before YAHWEH your EL. 32 It will be for you a Shabbat of complete rest, and you are to deny yourselves; you are to rest on your Shabbat from evening the ninth day of the month until the following evening."*

Purpose: This is a high Sabbath a day of fasting a means of cleansing our bodies. The Day of atonement therefore is a time of cleansing our bodies as well as that part of ourselves which is spiritual obligation to rest on the first day of Sukkot and not do any ordinary work.

Obligation to rest from ordinary work on the first day of Sukkot.

Vayikra (Lev) 23:33 *YAHWEH said to Moshe, 34 "Tell the people of Yisra'el, 'On the fifteenth day of this seventh month is the feast of Sukkot for seven days to YAHWEH. 35 On the first day there is to be a set apart convocation; do not do any kind of ordinary work.*

Purpose: It is a day in which we are to not be preoccupied. This is a time of rejoicing after coming out of the day of a set apart assembly of fasting. It is seven days of rejoicing. If there's a group, this can be a great time of eating and fellowship.

Obligation to rest and bring an offering made by fire and do no ordinary work on the eighth day of Sukkot.

Vayikra (Lev) 23:36 *on the eighth day (of Sukkot) you are to* have a set apart convocation and bring an offering made by fire to YAHWEH; it is a day of public assembly; do not do any kind of ordinary work.*

Purpose: This is the same as above. The end of this festival is a final day of celebration. The mitzvot defines the action to be taken.

Obligation to dwell in a Sukkah.

Vayikra (Lev) 23:42 *You are to live in sukkot for seven days; every citizen of Yisra'el is to live in a sukkah, 43 so that generation after generation of you will know that I made the people of Yisra'el live in sukkot when I brought them out of the land of Egypt; I am YAHWEH your EL.'"*

Purpose: To remember our ancestors once lived in sukkahs and witnessed the miracles of YAHWEH. We live in a black top environment. If one is able to put up a tent and reside in it for these seven days, then that is respectable. However, remember we are in exile we do what we are reasonably able to do.

Prohibition to curse YAHWEH.

Vayikra (Lev) 24:15 *Then tell the people of Yisra'el, 'Whoever curses his EL will bear the consequences of his sin; 16 and whoever blasphemes the name of YAHWEH must be put to death; the entire community must stone him. The foreigner as well as the citizen is to be put to death if he blasphemes the Name.*

Purpose: We are not to treat our EL in the same way as the nation's treat their gods. Blaspheming the Most High is characteristic of how one lives his life in unrighteousness. When we act contrary to the way the Most High El has given for Hebrew Yisra'el to live their lives; that is what it means to blaspheme his name.

The obligation to allow the land to rest.

Vayikra (Lev) 25:1 *YAHWEH spoke to Moshe on Mount Sinai; he said, 2 "Tell the people of Yisra'el, 'When you enter the land, I am giving you, the land itself is to observe a Shabbat rest for YAHWEH. 3 Six years you will sow your field; six years you will prune your grapevines and gather their produce. 4 But in the seventh year is to be a Shabbat of complete rest for the land, a Shabbat for YAHWEH; you will neither sow your field nor prune your grapevines*

Purpose: To allow the land to replenish itself. You should follow this mitzvot if you plant food or if you are a farmer.

Prohibition to exploit your neighbor.

Vayikra (Lev) 25:14, 17 *"If you sell anything to your neighbor or buy anything from him, neither of you is to exploit the other. 17 Thus you are not to take advantage of each other, but you are to fear your EL; for I am YAHWEH your El.*

Purpose: This is an ethical and moral mitzvot. It is an act that is just and right.

Obligation to support the poor.

Vayikra (Lev) 25:35 *"If a member of your people has become poor, so that he can't support himself among you, you are to assist him as you would a foreigner or a temporary resident, so that he can continue living with you. 36 Do not charge him interest or otherwise profit from him, but fear your EL, so that your brother can continue living with you.*

Purpose: This is moral and ethical and promotes harmony. We should do everything we can to help those who are poor in a way in which their lives would be deemed humane.

Prohibition to lend on interest to a Fellow Hebrew.

Vayikra (Lev) 25:37 *Do not take interest when you loan him money or take a profit when you sell him food.*

Purpose: To prevent the lender from gaining wealth by swallowing up the borrower's meager resources.

Prohibition to treat your Hebrew brother harshly.

Vayikra (Lev) 25:46 *But as far as your brothers the people of Yisra'el are concerned, you are not to treat each other harshly.*

Purpose: It is an act of moral, ethical, and just action toward our brothers.

Prohibition to make for yourselves any idols.

Vayikra (Lev) 26:1 "'You are not to make yourselves any idols, erect a carved statue or a standing-stone, or place any carved stone anywhere in your land in order to bow down to it. I am YAHWEH your El.

Purpose: To prevent idolatry.

Obligation to keep the Shabbats and revere the Temple.

Vayikra (Lev) 26:2 "Keep my Shabbats, and revere my sanctuary; I am YAHWEH."

Purpose: The Sabbath is for creation to rest so that what YAHWEH created could be productive. The Sabbath gives man, also his creation, the opportunity to rest in order to be productive. Man is EL's creation.

Contributions to the cohen.

Vayikra (Lev) 5:9 *"Every contribution which the people of Yisra'el consecrate and present to the cohen will belong to him. 10 Anything an individual consecrates will be his own [to allocate among the cohanim], but what a person gives to the cohen will belong to him.'"*

Purpose: The word Cohen means a priest who is also a teacher. If one desires to give to his or her teacher, it shall belong to the teacher. It is one's own contribution to allocate.

Chapter Summary/Key Takeaways

Tehillim (Psalms) 119: 97-100 *How I love your Torah! I meditate on it all day. I am wiser than my foes, because your mitzvot are mine forever. I have more understanding than all my teachers, because I meditate on your instruction. I understand more than my elders, because I keep your precepts.*

NOTES:

CHAPTER FOUR

APPLICABLE MITZVOTS – BAMIDBAR (NUM)

The obligation to observe Pesach.

B'midbar (Num) 9:1-3 *YAHWEH spoke to Moshe in the Sinai Desert in the first month of the second year after they had left the land of Egypt; he said, 2 "Let the people of Yisra'el observe Pesach at its designated time. 3 On the fourteenth day of this month, at dusk, you are to observe it—at its designated time. You are to observe it according to all its regulations and rules."*

Purpose: To remember the time our ancestors spent in Mitzrayim and YAHWEH's deliverance.

Obligation to keep Pesach in the second month on the fourteenth day.

B'midbar (Num) 9:10-12 *"Tell the people of Yisra'el, 'If any of you now or in future generations is unclean because of a corpse, or if he is on a trip abroad, nevertheless he is to observe Pesach. 11 But he will observe it in the second month on the fourteenth day at dusk. They are to eat it with matzah and maror, 12 they are to leave none of it until morning, and they are not to break any of its bones—they are to observe it according to all the regulations of Pesach.*

Purpose: This mitzvot allows persons who are not able to observe Pesach on this designated day to do a make-up because Pesach is a required feast.

Obligation to blow the trumpets on days of rejoicing.

B'midbar (Num) 10:10 *"Also on your days of rejoicing, at your designated times and on Rosh-Hodesh, you are to sound the trumpets over your burnt offerings and over the sacrifices of your peace offerings; these will be your reminder before your EL. I am YAHWEH your EL."*

Purpose: It is a reminder to YAHWEH of gratefulness. The sound of the trumpets/shofar are intended to help us focus on the events to which they are sounded. The trumpets/shofar are sounded at these events the sighting of the new moon, feast of trumpets, Shavuot, Feast of Matzah, Feast of Sukkot. These are designated times.

Obligation to observe the one Torah.

B'midbar (Num) 15:15 *"For this community there will be the same law for you as for the foreigner living with you; this is a permanent regulation through all your generations; the foreigner is to be treated the same way before YAHWEH as yourselves. 16 The same Torah and standard of judgment will apply to both you and the foreigner living with you.'"*

Purpose: It is the guide or governance for the Hebrew nation and those who are foreigners that join Hebrew Yisra'el. Its purpose is to provide order and stability for the Hebrew nation.

Obligation for the Cohanim to receive the tithe.

B'midbar (Num) 18:21 *"To the descendants of Levi I have given the entire tenth of the produce collected in Yisra'el. It is their inheritance in payment for the service they render in the tent of meeting."*

Purpose: Is to ensure the care of those who serve YAHWEH's people in exile. This mitzvot is germane to people who serve YAHWEH and the Hebrew nation. It is not for the nations and religious orders who do not follow the ways of the Most High EL. They promote the teaching of not being under the Law/Torah

Obligation to observe Feast of Matzah.

B'midbar (Num) 28:17 *On the fifteenth day of the month is to be a feast. Matzah is to be eaten for seven days.*

Purpose: The Regulation for observing the Feast follows in verses 18 – 25. Besides eating matzah for seven days and holding the two convocations the rest of this regulation is fulfilled in the Land. See mitzvah Vayikra (Lev) 23:6-8 explanation.

Obligation to observer Shavu'ot.

B'midbar (Num) 28:26-30 *"'On the day of the firstfruits, when you bring a new grain offering to YAHWEH in your feast of Shavu'ot, you are to have a holy convocation; do not do any kind of ordinary work; Observed in Exile*

Purpose: Shavu'ot is a day germane to celebrating two things. Primarily first fruits the first-gathered produce of wheat harvest.

Secondly the giving of the Torah to Hebrew Yisra'el. What's interesting is that none of the text speaks to this festival being related to the giving of the Torah. It just happens that they both fall on the same day. Therefore, Shavu'ot by text has no reference to celebrating the giving of the Torah. It is strictly germane the spring harvest. The giving of the Torah shows up days later in Sh'mot Chapter 34:10-28.

Obligation to observer Feast of Trumpets.

B'midbar (Num) 29:1 *"'In the seventh month, on the first day of the month, you are to have a holy convocation; do not do any kind of ordinary work; it is a day of blowing the shofar for you.*

Purpose: It serves to call our attention to the time of teshuvah (repentance) also rememberance. The shofar (trumpet) sounding is for the awakening for the high set apart season. It prepares us for the forth coming, Yom Kippur (Day of Atonement), which is very essential to the Hebrew nation. This is repeated from Vayikra (Lev) 23.

Obligation to observe the Day of Atonement.

B'midbar (Num) 29:7 *"'On the tenth day of this seventh month you are to have a holy convocation. You are to deny yourselves, and you are not to do any kind of work.*

Purpose: This is a high Sabbath a day of fasting a means of cleansing our bodies. The Day of Atonement therefore is a time of cleansing our bodies as well as that part of ourselves which is spiritual. This is repeated from Vayikra (Lev) 23.

Obligation to observe Sukkot.

B'midbar (Num) 29:12 *"'On the fifteenth day of the seventh month you are to have a holy convocation. You are not to do any kind of ordinary work, and you are to observe a feast to YAHWEH seven days.*

Purpose: Observing this feast time is a reminder of our ancestor's time in the wilderness when they lived in booths. We honor it by holding a set apart convocation. Where we are encouraged to pitch a tent and reside in it these seven days. However, Hebrew Yisra'el is in exile and grace is extended to our inability to fully observe this commandment. See the mitzvah in Vayikra (Lev) 23:33 for explanation.

Obligation to observe the day after Sukkot the Eighth Day.

B'midbar (Num) 29:35 *"'On the eighth day you are to have a festive assembly: you are not to do any kind of ordinary work.*

Purpose: The purpose of this mitzvot goes with the above explanation. Hold a convocation on the eight day to close out the feast of Sukkot. This is repeated from Vayikra (Lev) 23.

Obligation not to break a vow to YAHWEH.

B'midbar 30:3 *"Here is what YAHWEH has ordered: 3 (2) when a man makes a vow to YAHWEH or formally obligates himself by swearing an oath, he is not to break his word but is to do everything he said he would do.*

Purpose: This mitzvah is germane to deep thought on the part of the one making such a commitment. Making a vow or an oath should only be done with a sincere heart while understanding the gravity of the action being undertaken. Read the whole text of vows and oaths in this chapter.

Chapter Summary/Key Takeaways

Mishlie (Proverbs) 2:6-11 *For YAHWEH gives wisdom; from his mouth comes knowledge and understanding. He stores up common sense for the upright, is a shield to those whose conduct is blameless, in order to guard the courses of justice and preserve the way of those faithful to him. Then you will understand righteousness, justice, fairness and every good path. For wisdom will enter your heart, knowledge will be enjoyable for you, discretion will watch over you, and discernment will guard you.*

NOTES:

CHAPTER FIVE

APPLICABLE MITZVOTS D'VARIM (DEU)

Order to obey the mitzvot of YAHWEH.

D'varim (Deu) 4:1 *"Now, Yisra'el, listen to the laws and rulings I am teaching you, in order to follow them, so that you will live; then you will go in and take possession of the land that YAHWEH, the El of your fathers, is giving you. 2 In order to obey the mitzvot of YAHWEH your EL which I am giving you, do not add to what I am saying, and do not subtract from it.*

Purpose: To gain understanding and to follow the laws and rulings; and to prevent the corruption of the rules and instructions.

Do not become corrupt.

D'varim (Deu) 4:16-19 *Do not become corrupt and make yourselves a carved image having the shape of any figure—not a representation of a human being, male or female, 17 or a representation of any animal on earth, or a representation of any bird that flies in the air, 18 or a representation of anything that creeps along on the ground, or a representation of any fish in the water below the shoreline. 19 For the same reason do not look up at the sky, at the sun, moon, stars and everything in the sky, and be drawn away to worship and serve them.*

Purpose: To prevent idolatry and idolatrous worship.

Prohibition to make carved images of anything forbidden by YAHWEH.

D'varim (Deu) 4:23 *Watch out for yourselves, so that you won't forget the covenant of YAHWEH EL, which he made with you, and make yourself a carved image, a representation of anything forbidden to you by YAHWEH EL 24 For YAHWEH EL is a consuming fire, a jealous EL.*

Purpose: To prevent idolatry and idolatrous worship. Also, to prevent any thing or person from being worshipped besides the Most High. He is jealous for his people.

Moshe's admonition to Hebrew Yisra'el.

D'varim (Deu) 5:1 Then Moshe called to all Yisra'el and said to them, "Listen, Yisra'el, to the laws and rulings which I am announcing in your hearing today, so that you will learn them and take care to obey them.

Purpose: This admonishment is to all of Hebrew Yisra'el then and to this day. We need to remember the importance of study and devotion of our lives to the obedience of these laws and rulings of the Most High El.

Not to desire another's possession.

D'varim (Deu) 5:18 *"'Do not covet your neighbor's wife; do not covet your neighbor's house, his field, his male or female slave, his ox, his donkey or anything that belongs to your neighbor.'*

Purpose: To prohibit one from becoming preoccupied with desire for our fellow's property; and to prevent the possible outcome of theft.

Obligation to follow the entire way YAHWEH ordered.

D'varim (Deu) 5:29 *"Therefore you are to be careful to do as YAHWEH EL has ordered you; you are not to deviate either to the* right or the left. 30 (33) You are to follow the entire way which YAHWEH EL has ordered you; so that you will live, things will go well with you, and you will live long in the land you are about to possess.

Purpose: To be obedient to YAHWEH

The obligation to believe in the oneness of YAHWEH.

D'varim (Deu) 6:4 *"Sh'ma, Yisra'el! YAHWEH Eloheinu, YAHWEH echad [Hear, Yisra'el! YAHWEH EL, YAHWEH is one].*

Purpose: To solidify the oneness of the Most High EL as a core element of knowledge that Yahweh is the sole existent Spirit in the universe. Yeshayahu (Isa) 40:18 *Among whom, then, will you compare YAHWEH? By what standard will you evaluate him?*

The Obligation to Love YAHWEH.

D'varim (Deu) 6:5 *and you are to love YAHWEH EL with all your heart, all your being and all your resources.*

Purpose: The purpose of this mitzvot is evident. A person cannot fulfill EL's mitzvots unless one loves the Most High EL.

The obligation to teach our children.

D'varim (Deu) 6:7 *you are to teach them carefully to your children. You are to talk about them when you sit at home, when you are traveling on the road, when you lie down and when you get up.*

Purpose: It is through the knowledge of Torah that our children attain knowledge of the ways of the Most High EL. Without this teaching they will not come to know or understand the ways of the Most High EL. Without this teaching the child will not be able to function in right standing with the Most High El as it matures.

Obligation to put the mitzvots on the doorframe of our homes.

D'varim (Deu) 6:9 *and write them on the door-frames of your house and on your gates.*

Purpose: Placing a mezuzah on our doorframe acts as a reminder regarding one's knowledge of the mitzvots when one goes out and comes in. Note: You can google 'mezuzah' and find out where and how to purchase one.

Obligation not to forget we were slaves in Egypt.

D'varim (Deu) 6:12-15 *Be careful not to forget YAHWEH, who brought you out of the land of Egypt, where you lived as slaves. 13 You are to fear YAHWEH your EL, serve him and swear by his name. 14 You are not to follow other gods, chosen from the gods of the peoples around you; 15 because YAHWEH EL who is here with you, is a jealous EL.*

Purpose: To prevent idolatry and remain true to the EL of Yisra'el.

Obligation not to test YAHWEH.

D'varim (Deu) 6:16 *Do not put YAHWEH Eloheycha to the test, as you tested him at Massah [testing].*

Purpose: To always put the rules and regulations of YAHWEH to the forefront and obey what YAHWEH asks us to do. Obedience is the principal thing.

Obligation to diligently observe the mitzvot of YAHWEH.

D'varim (Deu) 6:18 *Observe diligently the mitzvot of YAHWEH your EL, and his instructions and laws which he has given you. 18 You are to do what is right and good in the sight of YAHWEH, so that things will go well with you,*

Purpose: Is to diligently obey. Understanding and obedience are key factors in maintaining a proper relationship with EL.

Prohibition to intermarriage with idol worshippers.

D'varim (Deu) 7:3 *Don't intermarry with them—don't give your daughter to his son, and don't take his daughter for your son.*

Purpose: Is to prevent idolatry from entering into the Hebrew nation of Yisra'el even in exile.

Not to derive benefit from idols and their accessories.

D'varim (Deu) 8:26 *Don't bring something abhorrent into your house, or you will share in the curse that is on it; instead, you are to detest it completely, loathe it utterly; for it is Set apart for destruction.*

Purpose: Is to keep Hebrew Yisra'el from falling into the idolatrous practices of the nations.

Obligation to not forget YAHWEH.

D'varim (Deu) 8:11 *"Be careful not to forget YAHWEH your EL by not obeying his mitzvot, rulings and regulations that I am giving you today.*

Purpose: As stated.

The obligation to fear YAHWEH, follow his ways and love him.

D'varim (Deu) 10:12,13 *"So now, Yisra'el, all that YAHWEH your EL asks from you is to fear YAHWEH your EL, follow all his ways, love him and serve YAHWEH your EL with all your heart and all your being; 13 to obey, for your own good, the mitzvot and regulations of YAHWEH which I am giving you today.*

Purpose: As stated

Obligation to circumcise our hearts.

D'varim (Deu) 10:16 *Therefore, circumcise the foreskin of your heart; and don't be stiff necked any longer!*

Purpose: To remove from one's heart thoughts and or actions which are a detriment to one's soul.

The Obligation to love the foreigner.

D'varim (Deu) 10:19 *Therefore you are to love the foreigner, since you were foreigners in the land of Egypt.*

Purpose: To treat every person who desires to join with you with respect always remembering that our ancestors were foreigners in Mitzrayim (Egypt).

The obligation to fear YAHWEH.

D'varim (Deu) 10:20 *You are to fear YAHWEH your EL, serve him, cling to him and swear by his name.*

Purpose: By fearing YAHWEH and having respect for his teachings one serves him and preserves the name of the Most High El amongst the nations.

Chapter Summary/Key Takeaways

D'varim (Deu) 4:1 *Now, Isra'el, listen to the laws and rulings I am teaching you, in order to follow them, so that you will live; obey the mitzvot of YAHWEH your EL which I am giving you, do not add to what I am saying, and do not subtract from it.*

NOTES:

Epilogue/Conclusion

While it is true that all of the mitzvots of the Most High El which he directed Moshe to teach to the nation of Yisra'el are written in most bibles. The true source written with clarity reside in the Masoretic text, the pure Hebrew properly transliterated. The Masoretic text clearly delineates who is speaking and does not use words such as Lord or God which confuses people causing them to believe Lord or God is a reference to the Greek's Jesus.

We learn from Scripture which consist of everything written in the Tanach, which comprise B'reshit (Gen) to 2 Chronicles in Hebrew text. These are the teaching and admonitions of the sole Creator of all things the earth and everything it consist of, the heavens and all it consists of.

The nation or Empire of Hebrew Yisra'el is in exile for its failure to obey the mitzvot of the Most High El. But in these exile nations Hebrew Yisra'el's obedience, to the laws and ruling, is the means by which it gains the protection and covering by the Most High El. All while being subject to the harshness of the nations to which Hebrew Yisra'el is dispersed.

Listen to the words of Moshe to this nation as he speaks from D'varim (Deu.) 4:5-8 *Look, I have taught you laws and rulings, just as YAHWEH my EL ordered me, so that you can behave accordingly in the land where you are going in order to take possession of it. Therefore, observe them; and follow them; for then all peoples will see you as having wisdom and understanding. When they hear of all these laws, they will say, 'This great nation is surely a wise and understanding people. For what great nation is there that has EL as close to them as YAHWEH our EL is, whenever we call on him? What great nation is there that has laws and rulings as just as this entire Torah which I am setting before you today?*

A key factor is knowing that because of one's obedience YAHWEH is near whenever we call. D'varim (Deu) 4: 7 *For what great nation is there that has EL as close to them as YAHWEH our EL is, whenever we call on him? 8 What great nation is there that has laws and rulings as just as this entire Torah which I am setting before you today?*

Finally, as you read through the Hebrew Scriptures you will find and see mitzvots which you may find applicable that are not enumerated in this text. Just remember YAHWEH'S golden rule OBEY!!!

Bibliography

Citing's and excerpts in this book are taken from David Stern's Complete Jewish Bible, and the King James Version

Acknowledgments

Many thanks to the congregation of First Tabernacle Fellowship for all their encouragement and support. Also, for your faithfulness to the teaching of the Most High EL. While many have turned away, you the remnant remained faithful to YAHWEH our EL. In the end of this day of grace and we enter into the Messianic Era your faithfulness will receive its reward.

About the Author

Rabbi Robert B. Holman, Jr. was from birth born into a Pentecostal Apostolic Jesus Only Christian faith. He attended local schools as well as the University of Nevada Reno. Rabbi began teaching and preaching the doctrine of the Apostolic faith at the age of nineteen and received full ordination in the Pentecostal Assemblies of the World organization.

In the Summer of 2006, a Hebrew text of scripture "this shall be a permanent regulation throughout all of your generations" stuck in his heart and the search for truth began. In 2007 Rabbi renounced the Christian faith and became Hebraic. By the inspiration of the EL of the Nation of Hebrew Yisra'el he came to the realization that that order of faith was going down the wrong path of worshipping and scriptural understanding.

Rabbi asked YAHWEH to teach him the truth of Torah so that those who followed the teaching might know the truth and gain eternal life through the word that is living and not dead. YAHWEH has taught Rabbi truth just as he taught Moshe that there is nothing more important to Hebrew Yisra'el than understanding his laws and teachings. After all, "TRUTH MATTERS." Rabbi's position is who shall we listen to YAHWEH and YAHWEH's Prophets or a people of Eurocentric persuasion who lack Hebraic truth and deny the Law of Moshe and continue in sin.

Made in the USA
Middletown, DE
08 November 2023